To
Magut

(handwritten signature/inscription)

The Heart Within:

Reflections on Zen Beyond Buddhism

by

Seijaku Stephen Reichenbach, Roshi

authorHOUSE®

AuthorHouse™
1663 Liberty Drive, Suite 200
Bloomington, IN 47403
www.authorhouse.com
Phone: 1-800-839-8640

First published by AuthorHouse 1/14/2009

ISBN: 978-1-4389-4152-3 (sc)
ISBN: 978-1-4389-4151-6 (hc)

Library of Congress Control Number: 2008911733

Printed in the United States of America
Bloomington, Indiana

This book is printed on acid-free paper.

Contents

Foreword

I am not an ordained priest, minister, or rabbi in any conventional use of such authorities. I was ordained by my community in 1975 to teach, to guide, to serve. It was ritual of trust, and I hope I have remained true to that trust. I have spent the last 33 years of my life trying to live up to that ordination, living the life of a monastic as I understand it. I teach what I teach because I have been able to do so as early as I can remember for reasons that are still a mystery to me. Others have referred to me as brother, mystic, spiritual pioneer, Roshi or Zen Master. I think I am just fortunate. I have always questioned all the accepted authorities as far back as I can remember. Each time I have chosen to look within myself, I have been graced with sight. When I look at the state of our planet and the human race, I don't know why there aren't more people looking, seriously questioning, and speaking too.

When you don't know who you are, when you have accepted the criticisms of others, as well as their social, religious, and political expectations as the sole authority of who and what you are supposed to be, you learn early on not to trust yourself, not to believe in yourself, and are left to rely on the authorities and dreams of others. You look everywhere outside of yourself for validation, approval, and any sense of power. This is not only a form of spiritual immaturity, but also the ignorance that Buddha, also called Shakyamuni, pointed to as the cause of suffering. I have never wanted to be anyone else but me as far back as I can remember. I have always held my dream for myself and the world to be as valid as and more necessary for me than anyone else's.

What I teach is freedom, and what I call Authentic Spirituality. Zen beyond Buddhism has been my vehicle. I am convinced that the purpose of your life, of anyone's life, is to live it and not someone else's idea of it, to achieve your own full capacity for being wholly and completely who you truly are. As George Bernard Shaw once wrote, you have the potential for, "Being a force in nature, rather than a feverish selfish little clod of ailments and grievances complaining that the world will not devote itself to making you happy." When you rely on authorities outside of yourself, you learn to expect the "world to devote itself to making you happy," and never realize the one and only real source for true happiness.

I wish for you that my words in this book will help you to begin to claim your birthright; to reawaken to your purpose for living; to begin to dream <u>your</u> dream again, and become a force in nature for healing our broken world.

Although the ideas in the chapters that follow are framed within some basic Buddhist concepts, I encourage you to think about Zen beyond Buddhism in a way that will enrich your own spiritual path, whatever that may be. I urge you to use what works for you in this book and trust your own heart, not simply relying on my own words.

Remember always, while you are reading, the truth is within you.

Seijaku Stephen Reichenbach, Roshi

Acknowledgments

First I wish to express my profound appreciation for the self-less service and labor of love given to me by Rev. Rachel Ninshin McCormick and Dr. Howard Enfiejian, whose sole devotion to truth, and service to me over the years, including the many hours of skilful efforts they applied to this endeavor made this book possible.

I thank my ancestors, my grandparents, aunts and uncles, whose spirituality was a function of their love for their family, for the earth, and for what this country represented to them in their lifetime. They taught me how to love life, how to labor and not just work, and to cherish every moment of life, every opportunity, every circumstance, and every situation. To my mother Rosina and my father Clarence who fed me, clothed me, and protected me in my youth, who sat up late hours into the night when I was ill, who worked, and worked, and worked – thank you.

To those who inspired me in my youth, guided me on my journey, and continue to guide me everyday of my life: Thomas Merton, John Fitzgerald Kennedy, Pope John XXIII, Pope John-Paul II, Mother Theresa, Werner Erhard, George Bernard Shaw, Shunryu Suzuki Roshi, Dainin Katagiri Roshi, His Holiness the Dalai Lama, and all my teachers, everyone I have ever met everywhere, everyday of my life. And last but certainly not least, my beloved friend and fellow monk Rev. Michael Shunryu Ginder and Rev. Mary Mutsumiko Schlembach whose faithfulness and endless service over the years keeps me vital and young – Thank you.

In the Beginning...

My Friends, There Will Be Suffering

What is the independent self-inquiry of Buddhism all about? Who was the Buddha and who are we -- we who dress in a certain way and do things the way that we do them, especially in a country that finds Buddhism so strange. Zazen -- or seated meditation that is intended to reveal impermanence, the unavoidability of pain, and emptiness -- is one of the three instruments of liberation in Buddhism. Zazen stands at the center of practice. It balances the virtuous life and wisdom. Zazen, virtue, and wisdom are the three instruments of freedom in Buddhism.

When we talk about freedom, you will find that we in the developed world have a very distorted sense of freedom. We have unfortunately come to believe that freedom means the ability to do or say whatever we want, regardless of the circumstances and situation. The true understanding of freedom is the ability to act with virtue, to act lovingly and kindly to others no matter how difficult it may be. The truly free person does not require life to be a certain way in order to respond with loving kindness in difficult situations. Truly free people do not require life to be a certain way in order to experience themselves as loving and free. Freedom from suffering was the exclusive objective of Shakyamuni Buddha. Why do people suffer? What is the suffering all about? Is it innate to life? Do we have a choice in the matter?

We cannot talk about freedom without talking about the noble truths of the Buddha. These are the foundations of our practice. The first words that the Buddha spoke at his very first teaching were, "My friends, life is suffering." The First Noble Truth is that there will be suffering. The Second Noble Truth is that there is a reason for this suffering. To understand the reasons for suffering leads to the Third Noble Truth, which is the cessation of suffering. There are certain forms of suffering that are innate to life, such as physical suffering and the natural decay of our bodies. But there are other forms of suffering. Fear is a form of suffering that drives many of our lives. Worrying in general, lack of confidence, worrying about tomorrow, worrying about being liked, worrying about money -- worry runs many people's lives whether they admit it or not. These types of suffering have a cause. When you understand what the causes are, you can begin to see the means for liberating yourself from suffering. Applying the causes for liberation is the Fourth Noble Truth, which leads to the cessation of suffering. Applying these truths to one's life will lead to being truly free – right here, right now. When we talk about being who we truly are, it is nothing we can imagine. However, we have experienced authenticity of self in our lives at least once. If you practice the teachings of the Buddha, you can experience liberation for the rest of your life.

The Buddha also taught that who we truly are is unlimited, pure potential. We are this truly loving essence, which the universe is. You have become convinced that you are limited in what you can be and who you can be and what you can do, but the truth of the matter is that none of that is true. What you are today is a function of that reality, and if you don't like what you are today, you can become anything you want. As Bill Gates might say, "Where do you want to go today?"

As the Buddha said, there will be suffering. The reason why there will be suffering is that we live in this kind of ignorance, this ignorance of who we truly are and what we may become. What is this? We've all asked this at least once in our life. What is life? What is the meaning of life? What is the purpose of life? Why am I here? The Buddha taught that the problem with our life lies in our not being in the here and now. Most of what we do, most of what we invest our emotions in, our lives in, has nothing to do with being right here, right now. The way that I often prove this folly to my students is that I give them an exercise. When you have your next clear night, a night when the moon and stars are shining, find a field or go to your own backyard, look up at the moon and the stars and let them know what you don't like. You will see the pettiness of the constricted world in which you live.

Apropos of this, a philosopher once wrote, "I experienced my initial freedom when I realized the benign indifference of the universe to my complaints." This is not meant to be sarcastic or facetious in any way. My intention is for you to see the reality that exists apart from our own little worlds, the worlds in which we hold an absolute belief. Because we believe that our little story is what life is all about, we miss out on the big story, the big picture. The core of the matter, whether you've realized it yourself or not, is as Saint Augustine once wrote: "Our hearts are restless until they rest in thee." I'm convinced that he understood that when we connect with the big story, we will be contented. It is our little stories that drive us to distraction. As Shakespeare said, most people's lives are like that of an actor who walks out onto the stage for a few moments, filled with sound and fury, signifying nothing. We live a brief moment, and then are gone. The moon goes on, the stars go on, the planets go on, the earth goes on. If every single human being were to disappear today, the earth would not only continue, but would be a lot better off.

You are to understand that the Buddha is not a deity, he's not a god. As Buddhists, we do not worship him and we do not pray to him. He has given us a path, a way that worked for him and has proven to work for Buddhas and Boddhisattvas since then. That is all. He was a man who, like you and I, had the very same questions that we have. Why do we suffer? What is the meaning of the suffering? Is there another way? And this is what he told us: yes, there is another way. Our suffering, for the most part, is our own doing. We are causing it from moment to moment.

Now, the problem in the West is that people get very upset when I say something like that. The difference between the East and the West is that we have bought into the beliefs of "bad" and "good." So when people hear that they are causing their own suffering, they get very unraveled about it. How can I be causing my own suffering? How could I have been doing this? I would like to make an observation that brings this to our attention very quickly: We can't even sit still. We can't just sit. We are always having to do do do, have more more more, be better better better, to gain gain gain. In the end, it is all just sound and fury, signifying nothing.

Another observation is that most people, in the business world especially, talk about the rat race. There's a reason why it is called that. If you buy a rat and intend to keep him in a cage, you buy him a wheel. The wheel is there for a very good reason. If the rat did not have the wheel, he would find a way to escape the cage. We put a wheel in the cage for the rat because when he is on the wheel he does not understand that he is not going anywhere. The rat truly believes that with the spinning of the wheel, he is going somewhere. The difference between rats and humans is that if you take the wheel away from the rat, he will become violent and try to get out of the cage. He will find a way. We believe in the wheel. We believe in the cage. We tend to stay in the cage with or without the wheel. People talk about living the rat race every day, with all kinds of activity, all kinds of fury, all kinds of effort. And in the end, we all pay our taxes, and we are all in the same place at the end of the week when we cash our checks. We are still thinking about the same things and wondering and worrying about tomorrow.

The wonderful message of the Buddha is that it does not have to be that way. He too realized his own rat race. He too realized that even a life filled with all kinds of wonderful possessions and pleasure would not be sufficient for him. He was a prince; he was destined to be a king and they rarely even let him walk on the ground. They carried him everywhere, they gave him everything he wanted, he had the life that most people dream of when they win the lottery. And yet, he found out that even that wasn't sufficient. He needed to know why. What he found out is that life is fundamentally a function of what we make it to be. It doesn't matter whether we are rich or poor. Freedom is not monopolized by anyone. Wealth will not do it; poverty will not do it. So there must be a middle way. And often Buddhism is called just that: The Middle Way.

When you begin to do zazen -- seated meditation -- you must do it in a way in which you are watching your thoughts and feelings. Just sit there. Or you can lie in your bed. But do not do it when you are going to sleep because then you will fall asleep. Do it especially when you have things to do. The reason why I say this is that most people think that seated meditation is difficult because of the posture that we have to sit in. I know people who have done it in chairs; I know people that have done it lying down; I know people who have done it in whirlpool baths. Everyone initially experiences the same difficulty. The difficulty is that we can't do it. We can't just sit. And if you take the time to do it, you will see that zazen has the power of introducing you to your life, because that is what zazen does. It introduces the practitioner to what is really going on throughout the whole day. Ordinarily, you don't notice it because you are constantly in motion. We are running, running, running and we don't SEE things. So when you go to a Zen monastery and just sit for ten minutes, what shows up is not "Zen practice." There is nothing "zen" about it to be honest with you; we're just asking you to sit still.

I tell people that my first Zen master was my father. He used to grab me when I was running around and say "JUST SIT STILL!" I did the same thing when I first started zazen as I did when I was a child. I squirmed around. And then my mind started going, "Why do I have to sit still?" Zazen is not this

"Zen" thing. It's not this Buddhist thing that you can try for ten minutes a day and then decide that you don't like it. It's not Buddhism. It's your life! Shunryu Suzuki Roshi used to tell his students that the difficulty with zazen had nothing to do with the posture or the time. It has to do with the fact that we are unable to keep what he used to call "beginner's mind." And what is that? The mind of a child. It is a mind that is open to possibilities. It is the mind of emptiness, the mind that is what this whole practice is all about.

Buddhism is about opening the heart. Our hearts have become closed and isolated from all other forms of life and from life itself. The practice of zazen and the practice of virtue and wisdom are powerful instruments that slowly crack open the shell and open the heart. This heart, the Buddha said, can do anything. It can sit for hours on end. When I first started this practice, I could not sit for five minutes without thinking and hurting and wanting to get up. Today I sit for hours on end. What has changed? Only my view of life, that's all. Nothing else has changed. I sit in the same posture; I do it the same way I did it thirty years ago. When the Buddha's successor came to his death bed and the monks were gathered around him grieving that he was dying, they asked, "What are we going to do?" The Buddha said, "Atta Dippa." Rely on yourself.

Throughout the Buddha's life, he said the same thing: don't just listen to what I am telling you today; try it. Find out for yourself. And that's the wonderful thing about this practice. It is that it's all up to you. I cannot give it to you. The Zen master is not some special being. You and I are Buddha. The difference between you and me is that I know that and you have yet to come to know that about yourself. That's all. The word Buddha means one who has awakened. Awakened from what? From the dream, from of the illusion that you can't, you can't, you can't and you have to, you have to, you have to, or else or else, or else. Wake up from the dream world that the Buddha spoke of. What the Buddha said to his students is that you have to do it for yourself. Do not rely on anyone else. Don't even rely on me. Just do the work. I have given you the tools; just go about the business of doing the work.

When we look at the causes of suffering, the causes of our own suffering, and the causes of suffering in the world, one of the fundamental teachings of Zen Buddhism is that everything that has form, everything that exists, is interconnected with everything else. That is to say, nothing happens randomly. Nothing. The problem that you dealt with yesterday, the blowup in the relationship, the dissolution of the relationship, the success of the relationship, did not happen randomly. Our experience of life, as Aldous

Huxley once wrote, is not what life does to you, but what you do with what life does to you. You have within you everything that the Buddha ever said in his lifetime, with everything you will need to be free. All the Roshi does, and all the Buddha did, was to give the means to the students. You must apply them. How you apply them depends upon what you bring to the moment.

Every one of us, me included, brings to every moment in life an idea about that moment. We go looking for that idea. Let's say that you go to a Zen center looking for something. You either find it and, if you do, maybe you'll go back the next time. Perhaps you didn't find what you wanted. Depending on how invested you are in what you wanted to find will determine whether you go back or not. It will determine whether you actually practice meditation or not. And this is the problem of life. We do this in our relationships. Ninety-nine percent of all difficulties in relationships have nothing to do with anything else but preconceived ideas and unfulfilled expectations. We bring expectations to every moment in life. Because of that, and because of our attachment to those expectations, there will be suffering. You know how people say, "Well, if your love is unconditional then…," and you'll notice that the person who is saying that always has a condition. The truly free person in any relationship is capable of the unconditional love that everybody craves. To live unconditionally, to love unconditionally, is to bring no expectations to the moment. I tell my students that it does not matter what anyone else does in the world. The only question you must answer is, "Who are you going to be in your lifetime?" You do not have a choice in anything else. You have the power to choose that and nothing else. Nothing else.

The Buddha said it this way: "When I look at all the forms of life, this is what I can prove to you -- everything is of the nature of impermanence." Everything I own, all of my possessions will rot and decay and eventually disappear. Every person in my life will age and die. I cannot truly say that anything is mine, except one thing: who I will be in my lifetime. That I do get to choose. The truly free person understands that. You and I have within us the capacity to be content at any moment. When I am content, no matter what is going on around me, I can now save the world. When I have developed the means of being content no matter what anyone else is doing, I can let them be.

When Martin Luther King and his followers were marching and being beaten and attacked by dogs and hosed down, he said to the police and the racists: We will wear you down. We will not hate you. We will not respond to your hatred. But we will wear you down. We will wear you down with our compassion. We will wear you down with our forgiveness, and in the end we will win and in the process we will win your hearts too. And they did. There is nothing more powerful in the universe than loving-kindness. But there is nothing more difficult to do if you have not trained yourself to do it. Pat Enkyo, who is a monk at the San Francisco Zen Center, speaks about this. She talks about the time before she was a student, when she hated the cops and the bigots and the racists and she thought that conflict was the way to overcome them. But she found out that the way to prove them wrong is what Jesus taught some 2000 years ago: to conquer the Romans would make me no different than they. War begets war, anger begets anger, hatred begets hatred and the only cure for that is loving-kindness. But one must know how to do it.

When the freedom riders in the sixties stood up against the most violent possibilities to attain their own freedom, they had to be trained. They had to be trained how to not respond with violence. And this is what the Buddha understood: every being is born with loving-kindness at the root of their lives. Why do you think everybody wants to be around a baby? They don't even have to know the baby. It doesn't even have to be their baby. Babies have the power of reminding us of who we used to be before we forgot who we were, to the time before we bought into belief systems and ideas about life. You see, babies live life directly. They experience the true nature of the universe. You did too. You weren't afraid of what people thought about you. When you had to poop, you just pooped. Today, if you pooped in public, you wouldn't be worried about the poop, you would just be worried about what everyone else thought. You see? Freedom is in just being. That's why everyone wants to be around a baby.

The Buddha way is, as many people phrase it, the means by which we "come home." We all want to go home, to that place where we are truly free to just be. But the path back is difficult. Practice is difficult. Anyone who tells you they have an easy answer is a liar and you should run away from them and stay as far away from them as you possibly can. It's not easy. Life is not easy. Life is suffering, but there is a way out of it. Many people have achieved it. Anyone can achieve it if they are willing to just do it.

In realizing my interconnectedness to all things, I can begin with my interconnectedness within my own body. Most of us tend to think that we feel the way we do in our bodies because there are external things happening that cause it. The Buddha said that what you think is what you will be, whatever that is. You will make your decisions accordingly. But the paradox of this teaching is that you cannot just walk around saying, "Ok, I'm Buddha, I'm Buddha, I'm Buddha." It doesn't work like that. We need to own our lives. When people come here to study Zen with me, they need to be prepared to take hold of their lives. When you sit with us in the evening, you will hear either me or a senior monk recite a prayer and the last line that we recite is, "Do not squander your life." This is a kind of admonition to practitioners to realize that life is gone in a moment. You never know when it will happen. On September 11th a whole nation, a whole world, got a taste of that. We had no idea of what was coming. In a matter of minutes, thousands and thousands of lives were changed forever. Life is like that. There is nothing more important than this moment, right here, right now.

Zazen and living the virtuous life, as the Buddha laid it down, couples with wisdom, which has to do with seeing the world as it really is. Wisdom has the power to awaken a person in a way that he or she tastes and smells and hears and feels life even when they are sleeping. We come to realize that all that is important is here and now and how I choose to live it. When my view of the word begins to change, I change. The only thing that can change me is my changing view of the world. This is what the Buddha way is about. It is about living my life once and for all. Living it. I don't mean the story that I call my life. I mean living life. To live life is to be in life as it is, every moment, every second. To be in it. When it is rotten, be in that. When it is fragrant, be in the fragrance. But be in it.

Mother Theresa, who I had the honor of meeting once, wrote that it doesn't matter where you live. If you find yourself living in a palace, live in the palace. If you find yourself living in the streets, live in the streets. Wherever you are, just be there. Then you will get a sense of what it truly means to be alive. And you will learn that it doesn't matter whether you are in a palace or in the streets. True freedom is a function of being able to be contented no matter the circumstance and situation. This is about responsibility. The word "responsibility" means to be able to respond to life. We talk about responsibility in this world like we talk about everything else. We don't know what we are talking about. Responsibility begins with a willingness on your part to live life as it is. You don't need to go home and throw things out. You don't need to change your parents. You don't even need to change your past. You don't even need to change. What you need to do is to recognize who you truly are right now, despite the clothes you are wearing or what you think you have become, or what you think you need to be. Be that and things change naturally.

So I invite you to first, become aware of the suffering in your life. The way to do this is to just sit. Just sit and watch what shows up. Watch your thoughts and you'll begin to notice what is driving you unconsciously.

When we talk about the unconscious, you have to understand that it is not some domain outside the universe. It's just what we're not aware of. People talk about miracles. All miracles are things we have just seen for the first time. Right now, under our noses at least fifty-two thousand miracles have happened. Haven't you seen them? That is all that change is. To be able to see what is right in front of us requires us to live our own lives. I tell my students that they need to give up judging at all levels. You cannot judge others and you cannot judge yourself. So, in the practice of beginning to own my life, I take it just as it is: all my mistakes, all my failures, all my successes, all my joys, all my accomplishments, and I put them in the same box. I call that box the me I love.

One of the thoughts that screw us up so badly is the idea that all we need to make us happy is to have all the good stuff of life. If everything were good and happened the way it should happen all the time, life would be great. But here is what we fail to recognize: we can't have the good without the bad. Otherwise, how are we going to know if something is good? When I say the word "up," your mind automatically thinks of "down." You think that it thinks of "up", but really it thinks of "down" because the only way it knows "up" is by referring to "down." We need to stop judging the bad and we need to stop judging the failure. In seated meditation, we learn how to work with these things. We allow the natural, pure potential force of the universe to do it for us. Do you realize that right now in your body, your heart is beating, your cells are working, your hair is growing, and you've got nothing to do with it? You've been alive for as long as you have and you've got nothing to do with it. Look at the seasons. Jesus would say, "Behold the lilies of the field and the birds of the air." They don't toil as you do. They don't worry like you do, and yet I've never seen a bird that is skinny or hungry.

The universe is pure potential with which we have lost our connection. The Buddha Way is the means by which we can reconnect with it. Now, here's the paradox: when I know who I am, I then know who you are, and you are no longer as scary as I used to think you were and neither am I. Now we can be friends. Now we can be who we truly are, brothers and sisters. Now we can learn to live together, believing in and protecting with our very lives the equality of all the many beings and the right of every single person to be free and to be happy. All beings are Buddha. This was the message of Shakyamuni Buddha and this is the true meaning of this Tathagata.

A Hall of Mirrors

What is practice? Specifically, what is Buddhist practice? As the foundation for our practice, we have zazen and the Four Noble Truths. So, what does Buddhism do? What is the way of the Buddha?"

It is the practice of opening our hearts.

I often mention the first Japanese roshi's when they arrived in the West in the early 1950s and later in the early 1970s. About half of them returned to Japan, believing that Buddhism would not work in the West. What I am pointing to is that the problem for each of us, especially in our modern society, has to do with the obvious, or maybe not so obvious, foundation of Buddhist practice: the First Noble Truth. What the Buddha wanted us to understand is that in life there will be suffering. In understanding our suffering, we find freedom. The problem in our society is that many people who take up the spiritual path have what the Buddha called the wrong understanding of practice. The first principle of the Eightfold Path as defined in the Fourth Noble Truth is Right View or Right Understanding. Right Understanding is that there will be suffering and that suffering is a part of life. As Buddhas, we are to view suffering very differently than our modern society views it. What do I mean by that? Many of us need to look at how this is true in our own lives, and not to see it in society as a whole. What we usually do with suffering is try to find ways of avoiding it. In fact, many people take on a spiritual life for that very reason. They believe that the path will help them feel better, help them to stay out of trouble, and help them avert suffering.

In fact, genuine spirituality is quite the opposite. The journey that will end up in the cessation of suffering for all the many beings is right through its graveyard of our lives, right through the suffering of our lives.

We cannot use a normal mode of thinking in our spirituality to avert suffering, to get around it or to deny it and avoid it. Any genuine spiritual path, any genuine religion, points to suffering as the heart of the matter. Buddha Shakyamuni's desire was to understand the human heart, to understand the human condition. When we talk about opening the heart, we need to understand the Japanese word "kokoro" or "the spiritual heart within." When we think of the heart, we automatically think of the heart in our body. The Japanese are pointing to something much deeper and more profound than just the physical heart itself, to something very deep within us.

The suffering to which I refer is worry, fear, lack of self-confidence, and our effort to make our lives safe and secure and be a certain way. Buddha looked deeply at suffering and said there is a cause for it. And because there is a cause for it, it is not necessary suffering like the decay and ageing of the body. It is important for us to understand this. Suffering, in whatever shape or form it comes in, has a cause. When we understand the cause, there is a means of transforming it within the heart. The best way to understand this is to recognize a fact of life that most of us do not want to admit and that most of us go through our lives never even realizing. At birth, we are born with an open heart. Infants are the evidence of this. They trust everything. Anything that comes along, they trust it. You did. They are open to every experience. They cannot get concerned about the things that you and I do. This trust lasts for all of us until we sold out. We entered a state of fear, a state of denial. We forgot how to have an open heart.

Somewhere in our lives, we entered into a sort of training to make us forget who we truly are. We learned this from society, from religion, from the world around us and from our experiences. So when I talk about experience, I talk about what we begin to do with life's circumstances and situations. We begin to discriminate and set away from ourselves anything uncomfortable because we fear it. We only bring to us what we consider to be comfortable and in doing that, we do not recognize that we have become addicted to feelings. We do not like to hear that. We have become addicted to only a part of life – the good times, the good feelings. We begin to spend the rest of our lives trying to find more of that. When those "good" things become dissatisfying, as they inevitably do, we begin to look for something different.

And when we have something different, we want more of that. We find ourselves trapped in the rat race.

If we were to wake up to the fact that we are only on a wheel called the rat race of life, we would do the work of tearing ourselves out of the box. Our problem is that we have come to believe in the wheel. We believe in the wheel of getting more, of being better and different because we have forgotten who we truly are. The Buddha taught that the three poisons are greed, anger (when used in the wrong way), and ignorance or a sort of apathy to life. These symptoms appear because we don't know who we really are and we don't know the true nature of life.

A Zen Master once turned to a student who was suffering and said to him, "Your problem is that you think you have time." You think you have time. The words of the teacher were pointing to the true nature of life. Everything is impermanent. Everything changes and once it is gone, it is gone forever. If we can learn to live our lives as if we don't have the time that we think we have, imagine what life would be like for us. Imagine all the things we would get done. Imagine, in the process of getting things done, we would develop self-confidence. The self-confidence that I have is a result of doing the things that I feared the most, of doing what I doubted I could possibly do without someone telling me how to do it or without somebody else doing it for me. In the context of impermanence, we don't have time. None of us knows when death will come. None of us knows how it will come. I remember when I went to my first funeral and I asked my grandfather why everyone was crying. He said they were crying because they failed to say things to that person when he was alive. That's why. They thought they had time. They thought they had time.

The urgency of life is one of the characteristics of the truly genuine spiritual practice. It is always urging us to get things done, to let go -- to let go and move on. When the heart opens, it understands this. It understands that the little dramas of our lives are not really worth the time and energy we invest in them. It understands that we should not be so concerned about what everyone else thinks because even if we succeed in meeting everyone's expectations, we are going to die. If we fail to meet everyone's expectations, we are going to die. There is a greater purpose in life than the service of the self. May we all use our suffering to serve that which is greater than ourselves.

In Tibetan Buddhism, there is the teaching that death is to be viewed as the great liberator. Just think about the lengths to which we go to avoid just speaking about death. Look at what we do when people die. We dress them and paint them to look as if they haven't died when what is lying there is a corpse. When the Buddha was training his monks to teach the Dharma (the teachings of the Buddha or the laws of the universe), he had them sit and meditate at grave sites. At that time in India they did not dig holes for bodies as we do. Look at what we do; we hide them.

We are to understand our physical death as a metaphor for the little deaths throughout our lifetime that we try to avoid. Everything is impermanent. Everything changes. Our own death points to this. Search yourself for a moment and answer this question silently. When you die, and you inevitably will, what dies? Two things. First, and most obvious, the body dies. Is there anyone who thinks that the body persists after death? In spiritual practice, we are to understand what the body is. What is its purpose? The Buddha taught that many of our physical illnesses are a function of treating the body as something other than what it really is. It is a temporary instrument of communication. It carries you through this life for a finite time. It is not designed to last. There is a reason for the impermanence of the body. We need to understand how to treat our bodies and how to live with them.

The second thing that dies is what you treasure more than anything else in your life. It is the thing you spend more energy in taking care of than anything else. It is none other than what I call your story. My story. Our story. That illusion. That ghost which we call ourselves. In Zen Buddhism we say that there is no self which I can call myself. The masters are pointing to the fact that the self which you talk about when you want to talk about yourself, is your story. When you walk up to people socially and ask them, "Hi, who are you?" the first thing they give you is their name. We know that your name is not you. We know that when you die, your name dies with you. Some of you think that you live on in the memories of others. That is true. But only for a short time. Those people in turn will die too. When all the people who remember you die, you are gone too. It may take a while, but that is the nature of impermanence. You can't trick the Dharma. The Buddha realized that something lives on. If you begin to do the work of discovering what this is, you can look at all of the things that you think you are. You can take a paper and pencil and write them down. Start checking off all of the ones which, when you look at them long enough, will disappear upon death. In the end, we are left with nothing. Whatever is on that list will be gone. Jesus tried to teach this to his students. When they arrived at Jerusalem and saw the temple, all of the disciples were awestruck. Jesus said, "Why are you so impressed by this? I promise you that one day not a stone of this will be left. It will all be gone." What he was trying to tell them was to focus on that which lasts after everything else is gone. When we understand the teachings of death in Buddhism we understand this: good life, good death; bad life, bad death. Think about it. If your lifetime has to do with things that are impermanent, think about what death is going to be like. Most people have difficulty facing death because they are afraid of it. Because somewhere deep inside, we know that all of the things we've devoted our lives to will be gone. What will be next?

Our practice is to realize that which is greater than the self. Those of you who have taken the precepts receive a Dharma name. The Dharma name is not just ceremonial. It is the responsibility of the Roshi to choose a name for the student according to what he sees in him or her. He looks beyond the story, looks beyond the impermanence and sees the eternal. That is how he finds a name for the student. When you know the translation of those names, you will find that those are the things that last. For example, my Dharma name is Seijaku. It means "pure tranquility." No matter how many beings die, no matter how many things disappear, pure tranquility will always be present.

The cause of suffering is that we live lives that have nothing to do with this. We live our lives as if we have time. We live out of harmony with reality. And what is reality? Everything is impermanent. You and I have been given thirty seconds to dribble the ball. If we don't do it, they will take it from us. This is true for all of us. So, are we living a life that reflects impermanence or are we causing suffering for ourselves and our families and our society by living a life opposite to that? How much of our lives do we spend trying to protect that which will disappear in the end? Something that I might ask parents is how much time do they waste with their children trying to demand things of them that will eventually change anyway? They could have just been present with them. How much of your life is driven by fear – fear of what could happen if you don't do this, that or the other thing? All of the times that we spend reacting to fear we could just as well spend smelling the flowers.

A genuine spiritual practice, whatever it may be, brings us back to the human heart. Jack Kornfield says that, when you are searching for a path to take, you must ask this question: Does the path have a heart? If it does, follow it. If it does not, don't follow it. When we talk about a path having a heart, it is about coming back to what is true, not to our ideas about it, to what is real, not to what we would prefer to see. We must work with the human condition.

There is nothing magical here. If anyone tells you that he or she has a magical spiritual practice for you and has things you haven't seen yet, then run away. The Buddha wanted us to understand that everything we need to know is already right in front of us. A mystery is only something that we have not yet opened our eyes to see. God has hidden nothing. You believe in the story that you tell yourself about yourself, but this story that you believe so fervently may not be big enough to see the light and what is in the light. When we go into a dark room and turn on a light, all it does is to reveal what was already there. The furniture does not show up with the light; it was already there. A genuine spiritual practice reveals what is already there. It does not replace anything; it does not substitute anything and most certainly does not fix anything. In nature, in this Tathagata, everything is just what it is. Our experience is just our response to it and our response is a function of what we attach ourselves to.

In the Second Noble Truth, suffering is a function of attachment and greed. What is greed? Greed is nothing other than wanting what we think we do not already have. But why do we think we do not have something? Because we don't know who we truly are. We live our lives as a function of what we have come to believe. The Buddha said on the day of his enlightenment that all beings are Buddha. All beings are pure potential. Nothing is lost and nothing is gained. Everyone right now is complete. We suffer because we do not know that. I ask my Christian and Jewish friends to think about this. God's final words upon creating the universe were, "This is good." Then religion came along and tried to fix all of God's "mistakes."

We have to learn the practice of being with our suffering. We have to stop thinking that there is something in Buddhism that will tell us how to not suffer. It's not that way. The Four Noble Truths dispel this illusion. The First Noble Truth: there will be suffering. The Second Noble Truth: there is a cause for suffering. The Third Noble Truth: there is cessation from suffering. The Forth Noble Truth: Nirvana, the kingdom of God, is at hand. In understanding the causes of our suffering and transforming these causes, we will enter Nirvana. How do we do that? By living in a way that is in harmony with what God created, not with our idea about how God should have created it, not our idea about how He should be with me, not our idea about how our children should act. When the four promises of the Boddhisattva's Vow were first recited in American monasteries, people walked out in throngs. The very idea of acting humbly and speaking respectfully to someone who says something nasty to us! The first thing we want to do when someone steps out of line is bomb the hell out of them. Look at the amount of money we spend in our country on the military. Now we're going to spend more. Look at the amount of money we try to spend on just learning to live with one another. Now we're going to spend less. And the Buddha would say," Why are you so surprised?" There will be suffering.

When we come to Zen, we come to relearn how to live life. You cannot mix oil and water together. No matter how much you shake them up, you cannot mix them together. When you understand this, you will realize that zazen will not cure a day of lying and killing. Our practice is not a supplement to our lives. It is meant to be a means by which we transform them. As our foundation, we have the Four Noble Truths. When a baby experiences discomfort, it sits with it. When it poops in its diaper, it does not have a problem with it. We do. Babies don't worry about your opinions of them. They are free. We need to look at how we live our lives and understand the causes for suffering. And finally, we must be each others' caretakers. Any alleged spiritual path that is not all-inclusive, that does not teach the practitioners their responsibility for all other beings, is not a spiritual path. It is just another delusion.

The Buddha's life is what we use as a model. The Buddha was motivated to leave his comfortable life and examine the nature of life when he saw other beings suffer. When he saw others being sick, when he saw other beings dying, when he saw other beings afraid, he could no longer live with his life as it was. He could no longer just care about his own selfish needs. In our understanding of the Buddhist teachings, compassion sets us free. Being compassionate towards ourselves and others is what sets us free. But we have to know how to be compassionate. We're not being compassionate towards ourselves when we live in denial, when we try to cover over our fear. Buddhism is not some pie-in-the-sky, idealistic religion. The Buddha was clear, as was Jesus that you will love your neighbor in the same way that you love yourself. They understood the human condition. To the degree that you love yourself, to the degree that you are able to have compassion for yourself, to that degree you will be compassionate towards others. Compassion begins with the self. It is manifested and realized in the work of taking up a path that frees you from fear.

When we say that everything is karma, we are saying that each of us has developed patterns in our ways of living. When we say that something is someone's karma, we are saying that a person has learned how to be a certain way in life. Do the work of looking at a path. Ask the question, "Does it have a heart?" If it doesn't, then transform it. If it does, embrace it fully. If you do not do this work, then you will repeat your old dysfunctional patterns. If you keep responding to life in the same way, you will get the same results. Compassion for yourself is mindfulness living, living each day with a code of life that has a heart. Use the Buddhist teachings as a point of reflection. Always ask yourself, "Does this have a heart?" Some of my students have misinterpreted Zen as saying, "If it works, do it; if it doesn't work, don't do it." They get to a point in their meditation where it becomes difficult, so they stop meditating. What the Buddha was actually saying is that if what you're doing has a heart and will ultimately liberate you, then keep doing it. If what you're doing does not have a heart and will keep you in chains and trapped in a circle of fear, then stop it! We all know that this is easier said than done. This is where meditation comes in. We say, as His Holiness the Dalai Lama would say, that there are three pillars of Zen practice: the moral life, meditation and the sangha or community of likeminded practitioners. We need to know these things more thoroughly and live them every day of our lives. As I tell my Christian friends, either Jesus really did what he said he did when he died for everyone's sins once and for all, and that we don't have to be so afraid or what he did was worthless. We have the same thing in Buddhism. Either the Buddha really did see what he saw and everything is already complete, or we're all just wasting our time here. Maybe my second-grade Catholic school teacher was right – I'm in a hell of a lot of trouble when I die. What can you do? <u>Wake-up!</u> You may find that the only problem you've got is that you think you have time.

It Has Always Been the Oak Tree

The purpose of Zen practice, insofar as Zen can be said to have a "purpose," is the perfection of character. To perfect something is to, in this case, become the Buddhas that we are born to be. There are many misunderstandings of the teaching that all beings are Buddha. To better understand the words of Buddha Shakyamuni, consider the seed of an oak tree. We know that within that seed is a giant oak. It is not destined to be a little pod. When nurtured correctly, it will grow to be the biggest and strongest tree in the forest. We can say that the oak tree is our underlying Buddha nature. If it is not nurtured and cultivated correctly, it will never reach its full stature. When we say that all beings are Buddha, it is not to say that everyone right at this moment has realized their full Buddha nature. It is not to say that there is no need for refinement or for perfecting one's character. We do not expect an infant to take on the responsibilities of an adult, yet we know that the child possesses vast potential, everything it needs to be a perfect manifestation of Buddha nature. However, there is no guarantee that an individual's particular incarnation will achieve its fullest potential. That is entirely up to the individual.

To say that one has realized Buddha nature is to say that one has, in fact, achieved his or her fullest potential, and is no longer at the effect of fear. Zen practice provides a method for doing this. Zen shows us that the knowledge, the wisdom, and the understanding to do this are already within each of us. The role of the teacher is to direct the student to transform ignorance into penetrating insight. It is wisdom that achieves Buddha nature.

This practice is only for people who are seriously committed to doing the work. The way of the Buddha is not for everyone. How do our own desires play into this? We can compare our practice to that of an athlete, a dancer or an artist who wishes to become the best. These seem to be three distinctly different activities, yet they are exactly alike in that the desire to achieve a perfect expression in any path is the same thing. As we uncover our true selves, we will discover unique manifestations of the self within us. Some of us will manifest Buddha nature as a dancer, an athlete, a teacher, a parent. The possibilities are endless.

For example, when I was very young, I sensed somehow that I was born to be a spiritual teacher, that this was my destiny. I think all of us have a quiet sense of destiny, of where we find the most contentment. This morning, I saw a wild turkey outside. I watched her from the practice hall (Zendo) window. This is not just a sentimental or emotional thing for me. It is much more than that. I have come to see that each being, each turkey, each squirrel, each rabbit, each dog, has a unique nature. As I was watching, I said "purity, purity." What I mean by this it that there was nothing pretentious, nothing artificial in the turkey's behavior, whereas human beings have a lot of manufactured behaviors. This is connected to doing what others want and not expressing our true nature.

People ask, "When will I act from my true nature?" I have learned from thirty years of practice and teaching Zen that such evolution does not come until we are finally sick of behaving as other than who we truly are. It is very much like my experience with cigarette smoking. When I was younger, I used to enjoy smoking. I was up to three packs a day. People told me to stop smoking, and I knew people who had died from cancer. It wasn't until I got sick one day from smoking cigarettes that I was able to put them down and never smoke again. So when you get sick of not being who you truly are, you will do the necessary work to realize your true nature.

Zen practice begins with this awareness of self. Who am I at any moment? Am I who I truly am or am I the product of my desires and other people's expectations? People who say that they do everything for everybody else are not saintly. The reason we do everything for everybody else is that we are afraid of being rejected or not liked by them. Mindfulness practice is being aware, moment by moment of when my actions or reactions are a function of fear, desire or wrong view.

To reiterate, the foundation of our practice is rooted in and built on our belief that all beings are Buddha. Why do we say this? Because it was the first teaching of the Buddha. The first turning of the Dharma Wheel of Samsara --

the cycles of death and rebirth -- came when Shakyamuni Buddha awakened and said, "All beings are Buddha." Nothing is lost and nothing is gained. He wanted us to understand that every moment is an opportunity to be the strongest and the fullest oak tree in the forest. If we approach our practice by saying, "Well, that is a nice belief, but there are circumstances that prevent me from doing this," then our practice becomes very difficult.

We must, as the ancients said, muster up a great doubt, in effect, of knowing that we do not know. In the vow of commitment, we say that we devote ourselves to "not knowing" as the source of all manifestation. That is to say, life and everything in it, is beyond understanding. Life will prove us wrong at every turn. Whether we see it or not, like it or not, life is a great mystery. Why? Because everything is impermanent. Everything is constantly changing. Change is the only constant in life. When the masters talk about mustering up a great doubt, they mean not to depend on our thoughts or feelings about anything. If you root your practice in thoughts, your practice will be difficult. More than that, you will not achieve your objective.

The Buddha spoke of the Eightfold Path for attaining enlightenment -- right effort, right view, right action, and so forth. I've already described wrong effort, wrong view, and wrong action. The only beliefs we have in Buddhism are the facts that we can see. It is all mystery. No one knows what happens after we die. But we do know that death comes, and that there is something after death, even if that something is nothing. Because of that, any conclusions that we can make about life are null and void.

In addition to the Eightfold Path, our practice is founded on the Four Noble Truths of Buddhism. Many teachers have concluded that if you can fully understand the first Noble Truth, then the three other truths become clear and all understanding is present. The First Noble Truth that I mentioned previously is that there will be suffering. This leads to the Second Noble Truth, that there is a cause for suffering. So, when the mind is engaged in grasping for beliefs there will be suffering.

Inherently, there is nothing wrong with life. The Buddha teaches that nothing is lost and nothing is gained. So, if you indulge questions and answers about what seems to be wrong, there will be suffering. Why? Because your apparent reality is not the true reality of the universe. If our daily living is an expression of our true nature, then there will be contentment. No matter what else is going, on there is contentment. Questions of why, how come, and what should I do cause suffering. This is because that restricted reality, that way of being, is a manifestation of the little ego mind and not big mind, not the reality of the universe. The only place where the universe is not perfect is in our minds.

There will be suffering. Suffering is the result of indulging unreal worlds, of entering what the Buddha called the dream world. We all know that when we are dreaming it seems very real. One of the by products of satori, or insight into the truth behind dualism and discrimination, is that you know that you are dreaming all the time. When I'm dreaming, I know that I'm dreaming. There are always two people in my dreams. There is me acting in my dream as though it were real, and there is me watching the dream as though I were watching an actor. The person in the dream thinks that it is really going on. Most of us are dreaming all the time. We dream of rights and wrongs. We dream of "shoulds" and "should nots." It's a state of mind. Enlightenment is another state of mind. It is a state of mind in which the dreamer has awakened and is able to distinguish between dream and reality. There is one reality. Everything else is a dream.

Our practice is to wake up from that dream. The practice moves us towards the one reality. I call this process cleaning up your mess. Whatever karma I have created while dreaming, I clean up. Practice is internal. The external parts of practice are there to support the internal practice. They are the means of supporting the internal and manifesting the internal in the world around us.

Delusion, the dream, is a kind of dilution. It is like adding things to dilute our experience, or to weaken it. Whenever we add our thoughts, our opinions or our feelings to an experience we have diluted it. Take a pure, clear glass of water. The moment you add anything to it, it doesn't matter what, it is no longer a pure glass of water. It doesn't matter what you add to it. Add goodness to the glass of water and you have still diluted it. Add one grain of sugar and it will never be the same again. Illusions are anything from the world of impermanence. We are living an illusion when we think that life will last. It does not. The illusion is that the universe is not perfect and we have to fix it.

Now I want to talk about right practice. The Four Noble Truths are the foundation of our practice, so we know that there will be suffering. If you have not seen <u>The Lord of the Rings</u>, you should. There are several times in the movie where the wise characters make statements about man. One of the statements is that we will always fail when it comes to perfecting our reality. One of the reasons that we will always fail is that we believe in desire. Greed and the belief in answers are the reasons we will fail. The suggestion that we are greedy is offensive. We prefer not to think of ourselves as being greedy.

We need to know that the moment we desire, that is greed. The moment you make a desire, the purpose for anything is greed.

The Buddha taught that there are three poisons, three things that poison life: greed, the indulgence of anger, and folly. The Buddha spoke about how, if we indulge these things, there will be suffering. The Buddha also talked about necessary suffering. Inevitable suffering. Our bodies decay and get ill. But much of our suffering is manufactured. Our attitude plays an important role in this. Medical science, like never before, is taking a serious look at what the Buddha spoke about 2500 years ago: the connection between the mind and body. One's attitude, one's point of view, does affect what goes on in the body. All illnesses, aside from the natural decay of the body, are a function of one's attitude. When we talk about natural death, we mean that our bodies do what they are designed to do. Other diseases, including cancer, are a function of one's attitude. Let's see how that might work. If I am greedy, if I am always looking for something outside myself to make my body better, to make my life better, what is the message I am sending to my body? I'm telling my body it is weak, it is susceptible, it is vulnerable and not capable.

The Buddha was very clear 2500 years ago that if we perfect our minds, our bodies will follow so that when we die, it will be a natural death. I remember when my grandmother was dying not so long ago and my father wasn't accepting it very well. He kept bugging the doctor and bugging the doctor, and finally the doctor said to him, "You know, Clarence, she is 97 years old. The body was not built to go very much longer. It's natural for her. The body is shutting down. It's getting ready to leave."

Smell the coffee.

So what is right practice and how do we develop right practice? The three pillars of Zen practice are the Buddha, the Dharma, and the Sangha. To take refuge in the Buddha is to take refuge in the practice of zazen. The Dharma is the teaching of the Buddha. The Sangha is the community. All three are different manifestations of the same instrument. What is the Sangha? The Sangha is where we learn to perfect the virtue of bodhichitta. Without bodhichitta, no satori is possible. Bodhichitta is a genuine, altruistic concern for others. It is the compassionate concern for others. If there is no compassion, which is characterized by taking care of other people, and the forgetting of oneself for the benefit of other people, there is no satori. But here is where the paradox lies. Bodhichitta begins with oneself.

The problem with understanding bodhichitta is that most of us do not know the difference between pride and a genuine love for oneself. Pride is arrogance about oneself, where we feel that we are better than others or that we are more important than others. With pride there is a constant taking care of oneself at the expense of others. To have love for yourself has to do with an understanding of what this body, mind and heart need and of attending to that. This is why, when we eat food, we say that we accept this food so that we can continue our practice for others. I take care of my body; I take care of my attitude; I take care of my heart's necessities so that I can practice the Dharma. I want to read a quote to you from St. Francis De Salles:

"Be patient with everyone, but above all, with yourself. I mean, do not be disheartened by your imperfections but always rise up with fresh courage and gladly make a fresh beginning daily. There is no better means to attainment of the spiritual life than by continually beginning again and never thinking that we have done enough. How are we to be patient in dealing with our neighbor's faults, if we are impatient when dealing with our own? He who is fretted by his own failings will not correct them. All profitable correction comes from a calm and peaceful mind."

All profitable correction comes from a calm and peaceful mind. To this end, D.T. Suzuki's thoughts are relevant:

"When you are practicing zazen meditation, do not try to stop your thinking. Let it stop by itself. If something comes into your mind, let it come in and let it go out. It will not stay long. When you try to stop your thinking, it means you are bothered by it. Do not be bothered by anything. It appears that something comes from outside your mind, but actually it is only the waves of your mind, and if you are not bothered by it, the waves gradually will become calmer and calmer. Many sensations come, many thoughts or images arise, but they are just waves from your own mind. Nothing comes from outside your mind. If you leave your mind as it is, it will become calm. This mind is called big mind."

Another philosopher said, "I became free when I realized the benign indifference of the universe to my complaints." Many people don't like that because it sounds offensive. The reason why God or his universe doesn't care about us is that God sees things from God's point of view, not from our point of view. In God's view, there is no beginning and no end, so what's the problem? What are we afraid of? The Heart Sutra -- a prayer whose theme is "form is no other than emptiness, emptiness no other than form" -- says: if no birth, then no death; no beginning of life, no ending of life; none of those things. So, do you see why God doesn't really care about your complaints?

You can see why big mind is calm at all times. It's only little mind that gets concerned and upset.

If we use these teachings, we have the foundations of practice or at least the foundations of bodhichitta, a genuine altruistic concern for others, which begins with ourselves. For example, would you be satisfied if you were told that you are to go to someone you love and care about and spend the day beating them with a stick until they are hurt so badly that they are afraid, that they are crying and that their life is disrupted? Of course you wouldn't. Then why do you do it to yourself? Possibly your lack of compassion for others is rooted in your lack of compassion for yourself. How can you expect to feel compassion for others if you do not feel it for yourself?

A paradox seems to arise here. We are not to be concerned about certain thoughts and sensations but we are not to act on some of them. It sounds like a contradiction doesn't it? On the one hand, we are not to be concerned. On the other hand, we have taken vows to act a certain way. How do we do this?

What we experience outside of us is a manifestation or an expression of what is going on inside of us. In the Buddhist way, we do certain things on the outside to reinforce something on the inside. How do we do that? By doing things on the outside according to the inner practice. Both are supporting each other. The outer and the inner. One is never in opposition with the other. So act compassionately, act altruistically and you will develop that within yourself. Treat yourself compassionately and treat yourself altruistically and you will develop that for yourself.

Here's an example. It might not seem to be spiritual, but it is. From the time I was very little; my father was giving out his secrets for financial success. Certainly in his lifetime he has achieved it. We define financial success as freedom, the ability to come and go as we please. One of his rules for achieving financial success has been: every other week, before you pay anybody else, you pay yourself. What does that mean? Every other week he put money away for himself, taking care of his dreams. So if you want to try that, go ahead and see where you will be at his age. My friend Mr. Fitzgerald used to say it another way: One hand for the ship, and one hand for yourself. Because in a storm, if you go down, what happens to the ship? The ship goes down. And if the ship goes down, what happens to you? You see? Not two.

The practice of bodhichitta begins with a compassionate way of being with oneself. Whenever a sensation shows up, pay no attention to it. I don't care what it is. You are who you are. You are who you have vowed to be.

You are Buddha. Even though you have not realized your Buddha nature, you know innately how to be Buddha. You have the teachings on how to be Buddha. You are not to judge others; therefore you are not to judge yourself. You are not to be hateful towards others; therefore, you are not to be hateful towards yourself. You are not to be resentful towards others; therefore, you are not to be resentful towards yourself. You are not to make one thing better than other things. Therefore, whatever thought comes into your mind, let it come. If you will allow it to come, it will go away. That's what it does. That's what everything does. Everything comes and everything goes. Including you.

There are different forms of meditation. There is seated meditation, mindfulness meditation, the meditation of action, and so forth. Feelings come up. Watch them. Do you have to act on them? Not necessarily. But if you act on them, act on them effectively. If you act on something ineffectively, what have you done to it? You have altered its true nature. In aikido, we do not go against the energy of another person. We go with it. It doesn't matter from what direction the energy is coming; if we are prepared, and go with the flow, it will come and you will allow it to go. But what we tend to do, is to grab it and to throw it down and to hold on to it. That takes energy. If you ever see true masters of the martial arts at work, they barely break a sweat. And there you are here huffing and puffing with the heart rate of 270 saying, "Life is suffering!"

When you truly understand that everything is complete as it is, lacking nothing, you do not need anything. All enemies disappear, all worries disappear. And there you are, looking very strange to everyone else in the world. But even that doesn't exist for you. You see everyone out there in the world looking at you, but you know who they truly are. And you laugh because they are actors. When you go to a play, you understand that it is not real. That is what life is. It is a comedy. Look at it. Everyone goes around buying these big houses and fancy cars and then they spend their whole life to keep these possessions, working, working, working and then they die. Then they can't keep any of it anyway. We go to church and we pray. We say, "God, please make this all better." And God says, "What do you mean make it better?" God doesn't understand better. Better does not compute with God. You have to know how to talk to God in God's language to get a response. I hear God all the time. We have good talks, he and I, even if he's a she or an it. God could show up in drag, and I wouldn't care. We know innately how to be.

In the practice of bodhichitta, we allow thoughts and feelings to show up and we act in a certain way. When people ask why you act this certain way, the only effective answer is, because I said I would. The moment you say, "Because it's the Buddha way," you've lost it. In satori, there are no Buddha's, no sentient beings, no enlightenment. None of that exists. In God's world none of that exists. This is to be understood as effective practice. This way is only for those who desire to achieve awakening and full realization of their true nature. It is not for anyone else. All others need not apply. The foundation of this practice is that nothing is lost and nothing is to be gained. It is already complete as it is. All of this stuff showing up within you, all of these feelings and thoughts mean nothing. All of them. You need to be careful. I'm not just talking about the bad feelings. I'm talking about the good ones too. I'm not just talking about the uncomfortable ones. I'm talking about the pleasurable ones too. Look what we have done to a good time. We don't even know how to have a good time! Anyone who does not know how to eat and drink and have a good time will never achieve satori. You see? What matters is that we do these things effectively. You will love others as you love yourself.

There is no other way.

As Nike Buddha says, "Just Do It"

Let go. Just let go. When we do this, when we really do this, we understand that we have no real control over anything. Eihei Dogen Zenji, the founding patriarch of the Soto Zen tradition in Japan, had a few things to say about letting go. Dogen said that Zen is the study of the self. He goes on to ask how we study the self. We study the self by forgetting the self. As Zen students, we believe that all knowledge, all real knowledge, is experiential. However, the Buddha said that most of us live as if we were in a trance, in a waking dream of sorts. This is analogous to hypnosis, where the subjects awaken and remember nothing of what they said during the trance. Similarly, we often can't believe that we've done the things we've done and said the things we've said. We were in a "trance" at the time. To this end, I'd like you to look at something. When we study the self, this self that we call "myself," what do we really mean? For years, my students have heard me say that when we look at the self from the perspective of Zen practice, we see that the self is a bundle of thoughts and feelings. They are what we present to people when we are referring to "ourselves." What are we presenting? We can sum it up in this way: This self you call yourself is first of all a set of feelings. Most people, when they talk about themselves, are talking about their feelings -- how they feel about things and whether their feelings are where they would like them to be or not. This self that I call myself is also a set of thoughts. When people are talking about themselves and presenting themselves to others, they will typically say, "I think" or "My opinion is" or "My belief is" or "The way I think it should be done is this way," and so forth.

This self is also a collection of memories. They are the resources that we use to make decisions in much the same way that a computer uses its data base to generate output. Memories refer back to something. They could be events in your life, things that you learned one way or another. A problem arises when the self identifies with these memories, with the phenomenal world. So, this self I call myself is for all practical purposes a collection of thoughts and feelings and memories.

Let's look at these thoughts, feelings, and memories because they dominate the self. One sense in which we talk about our memories is to affirm a thought, to celebrate something or to indulge a feeling. The opposite can also happen. Memories can ignite within us a certain set of thoughts or a certain set of feelings. When we think about the "good old days," certain feelings arise. When we think about a terrible thing that happened last week or 9/11 or the death of a loved one or something like that, a different set of feelings will arise. What always accompanies our indulgence of memories are feelings and thoughts. We can say safely, without any doubt, that for at least 2500 years, all Buddha's have spoken about this self, pointed it out to their students, taught them how to study it thoroughly, and have them realize that this "self" that I call "myself" is a transient aggregate of feelings and thoughts.

So, what do we know about feelings and thoughts when we look at them? Sometimes we're happy. Sometimes we're sad. Sometimes we feel safe and secure. Sometimes we feel fear. We could go on and on with this, but finally one thing we can say is that thoughts, feelings, and memories are all unstable. They are never constant, never consistent; we're never always happy and we're never always sad. It's the same with security and fear, the same with our thoughts. Mohammed Ali once said, "A man who reaches 50 and sees the world the same way he did when he was 20, has just wasted 30 years." It always holds true. I didn't see things in the same way when I was 20 as I did when I was 2. If I did, I would be in a lot of trouble today.

Now let me ask you this: if you had the choice as to what thoughts and feelings would be present in your mind, how many of you would choose constant sadness? How many of you would choose constant insecurity and fear? So can we safely say that, in the domain of self, you have no choice? But we know that if you had a choice, you would choose happiness. Can I safely say that you would go to great lengths to keep it that way? How many would choose maliciousness as opposed to compassion and loving kindness with those people in your lives? Could it be that what Dogen was saying is that the self you call yourself is not really you? If you had it your way, you would choose joy and love and kindness and happiness. So Dogen said the way we study the self is by forgetting it.

How many people have had mornings when they wake up feeling great, and mornings when they wake up feeling like crap? Then they ask, "Why am I feeling this way?" How many of us have had the experience of loving someone clearly and profoundly and, the next moment, of wanting to tear them apart with words? And there it is -- the you that you try to avoid most of the time. Is it possible that this self that we call "myself" is not the true me? Most definitely. I am convinced that, somewhere in our lives, we were all hypnotized into believing that this inconsistent self is who we are. If we weren't, how can we explain why we go to such great lengths to protect it when it feels threatened? What happens when someone doesn't like your opinion, someone doesn't like what you think? You get really upset about it. At the very least, you start to doubt yourself.

I like to talk to high school students. It seems as if they understand this a lot more than adults do for some reason. I start by telling them that the most important thing they need to know – and if they don't know this they won't understand anything else -- is that we're all going to die. So I ask you, if we are going to die, that no matter what we do we're going to die, then what are we afraid of? What is it that we are afraid of? We know that our opinions die. Certainly my opinions of the world when I was two are not still around. This "self" that we've become hypnotized into relying on is unreliable. To see that and to learn how to practice what Dogen called "forgetting the self" on a daily basis, what some of you may call "letting go," is the key to freedom. As I have suggested to students and others with whom I have spoken, when you start to study the self, you start to see other things about it that aren't very nice. We start to understand that feelings and thoughts manage us – not the other way around. We talk about what <u>we</u> feel. We talk about what <u>we</u> think. But the truth of the matter is that I have no thoughts and I have no feelings. Feelings have me. Thoughts have me. Now, most people wouldn't get up in the morning if the thought caused by the alarm bell didn't get them up, would they? There is one thing on which we must be absolutely clear. We are not disparaging thoughts and feelings because, for instance, if we don't have feelings of fear at the right time, we are in a lot of trouble. Zen is not the substitution of one way of being for another. Buddhism calls upon us to learn how to balance both realities. That is why it has been called The Middle Way.

The self is always going to be with us and it has its uses. Without it we will not go and get food when we are hungry. Without it we will not run away from danger. We need it. It is perfect by nature. It was designed to protect us and to help us survive. But here's where the hypnosis arises. Somewhere along the line we became convinced that the survival of this self is an end in itself. Animals understand the proper use of the self. I have yet to see a gathering of squirrels discussing the day ahead, and so forth. They don't use the self for that. They use it for what it was designed for. When it is winter, they know what to do. Something in them, their self, tells them that. But somehow human beings come to believe that their thoughts and feelings, which are designed to help us survive, are who they truly are. Many people have told me that, if they had a real choice, they would seldom follow the directions of their thoughts and feelings, especially the ones that conjure fear, anger and malice. In this way, we know that something else is present within us. We can see this thing if we look closely enough. That something is the True Self. In the midst of this impermanent world there is a presence, a something. It is who you truly are. I'm not going to tell you what it is. You have to find that out yourself. No one told me what it is, so I am not telling you. It doesn't work that way. My teachers made me find it; now you'll have to find it.

To see this and to begin to practice this on a daily basis is where all genuine spiritual practice begins. First you must, as the Dalai Lama and the Buddha's have taught, discover the causes of suffering. The first cause of suffering is the reliance on things that are unstable and impermanent. If a man builds his house upon sand and the rains come and the house collapses, he's got nobody to blame but himself. The self is like sands pounded by water. It comes and goes. We never know what's coming next. Do we ever really know the next feeling that's coming? How about thoughts? When we begin to meditate, we see this clearly. Thoughts are flying in and out of us all the time while we are sitting in meditation. The same things occur with feelings. They come from nowhere. How many of us have gone through the day and someone says, "Where did that come from?" when we speak impulsively. Look at what we do sometimes with the people we love when we don't get our way or feel threatened. Later on, we may wonder, "What was that all about?" These are good questions. They help us begin to see what Dogen wanted us to see when he said that Zen is the study of the self. How do we live with that? My students have often heard me say that you need a purpose in your life greater than yourself. You need a purpose in your life greater than yourself in order to study the self.

For me, my overriding purpose is the freedom to be. I referred to the fact that we all will die. In my case, everyday death is a pervasive presence. It is not something I only think about when someone calls and says, "so and so is dying" or "I'm going to a funeral" or "will you officiate at a funeral?" Death is something that is present for me every moment. None of us know when it will come. Ask anyone involved with 9/11. The most important lesson of 9/11 is not how to upgrade our nation's security. Rather it is the urgency of living life fully here and now. Right now. The survivors learned to live life fully for their loved ones. Their whole attitude toward work is different. If employees feel the need to go home to attend to their children, bosses are now letting them go home and do that. September 11th was a rude awakening if ever there was one. People kiss their husbands and wives and children goodbye in the morning, assuming that they will come home that night. We take it for granted. It's just another day. Now, all of a sudden, it's a whole new day.

So, to study the self and to practice this forgetting that Dogen talked about is a goal for living that is bigger than ourselves. For Buddhists, it is a code for living in which we say, "However innumerable all beings are, I promise, I vow, to love all of them." We also say, "However inextinguishable desires may be, I vow that I will work to extinguish them all." And when we get to the end of these vows, we say, "However endless, these Dharma teachings are, I vow to master every one of them." This is impossible. Why would the Buddha demand the impossible of us? It was a ploy that he devised so that we understand that every moment of our lives is urgent and to stay awake. Practice is every moment. Do not for one second take the people we love for granted. They may not come home one day. You may not come home one day. Do not take your bodies for granted. They are the vehicles that will get will get us through life to be with the people we love.

I love it here at Pine Wind Monastery. I love the blue sky, I love the green trees, I love the people that come to be with me. People think, "Well, you become enlightened and then nothing matters." No. You become enlightened and <u>everything</u> matters. What always confronts us is the urgency of living in the moment. So how do we live in the moment? By saying that we will love, love unconditionally, act in concerned, compassionate ways for the sake of all beings. What if someone makes us angry? It doesn't matter. What if he or she hurts us in a way that justifiably provokes our anger? It doesn't matter.

True freedom lies in the ability to be who you say you are going to be no matter what anyone else does. That takes practice. It takes daily meditation where we discipline the mind to stay focused right here and right now and not wander off to the past or the future, which are illusions anyway. This takes the practice of patience. People say, "When am I ever going to be patient?" We're never going to be patient all the time. We need to know that we're going to be unconditionally patient when pigs fly. It doesn't work that way. What we need to do is to BE patience. We need to BE patience every day. Patience. What is it? Some people think patience is not being disturbed by anything. No. That's not what patience is. Patience is choosing to bite our tongues, choosing to refrain from harming others when we want to put our fists through their heads. Do you ever hear anyone talk about life as a script? In a way they know what they are talking about. What they are referring to is not necessarily acting, but in a way it is. When the director says, "ANGRY!" we become angry. We do it without thinking. When the director says, "FRIGHTENED", we're frightened. We're like an actor in a Shakespearean play, "who struts and frets his hour on the stage and is heard no more." We have our cues and we act them out.

Truly free people feel anger, feel frustration; but they breathe deeply, remember who they are, and then act accordingly. They choose to be compassionate and kind. This works only when we begin with ourselves. If you plan to study Zen and meditation, you will need to be patience incarnate. If you plan to live according to a purpose greater than yourself, you will need to be patient. It takes practice and it takes time. Sometimes it's a whole lifetime; or two; or three. We need just to choose that. We've fallen into a deep sleep, and it's going to take awhile to see that all those dreams of lacking and failing and not being good enough are just that. They're dreams. But the more and more we practice forgetting the self, when those things come up we forget them. "Forget it," Dogen said, "just forget it." It doesn't mean anything. As the Nike Corporation says, "Just do it." It's not easy to run two miles every day, so "Just do it."

Nothing that has ever had any value in our lives, if you look at them, as I have looked at my own, was easy. The easy stuff is fun and feels good while it lasts, but what really has the power of changing us, of teaching us, and causing us to grow is the difficult stuff. When circumstances call for us to give a little more than what we were prepared to give, we learn something about ourselves. We can get through it. We've all been near death when someone special died and we thought, "What are we going to do now?" And we find out, as they said in Terms of Endearment, "Not only do we survive, but we are stronger because of it." We do survive and we will become stronger because of the taxing things. So we must trust that everything is Buddha. One of the recitations that we perform is called the Bodhisattva's Vow. In the Bodhisattva's Vow, when someone is malicious towards us or when someone is even abusing us and cursing us, we vow with the humble but reverent belief that he or she is an avatar of Buddha who is training us to see that we don't have to rely on anything outside of ourselves. We are already Buddha's. When we practice that long enough, we begin to find out that we can have different opinions, we can disagree.

Let us rely on ourselves. Let us first learn a little more about that self. And the way we do it is by first discovering that this self that I call myself, as Dogen said, does not exist. It never did, it never will. It's time to go home and say hello again.

I would like to close with a cautionary tale of sorts. In taking care of ourselves, we must take care of the Earth, our mother. Our mother is ill. We have neglected her, we have forgotten her, and we have taken her for granted for everything that she is. Recently, the monks and I woke up and drove to our office (we work for a living). We often have the pleasure of seeing a family of ducks across the street and one morning someone had hit one of them. I don't understand how you hit a duck, I really don't. But someone had managed it and it was a day of mourning for us. Apropos of this, one of the things that living in nature has done for me is that I now drive the speed limit. It's not because I'm concerned about being stopped by a cop. I haven't been stopped in thirty-some years. I do it because wildlife is everywhere. Deer and other animals cross streets all the time. They have taught me how to slow down my car and they have also given me the opportunity to see them. And you know what? They are no different from you and me. No different. I often wonder who is in the woods watching who had just been hit.

I want to share with you another poignant incident. My family has a cabin above Williamsport, Pennsylvania. One day, when I was a boy, I was driving back to the cabin with my father. It was hunting season. We were driving down Route 15 past a farm and he pointed to a herd of deer coming down the hill. They were in a rush; they were running. We were both curious as to why when we saw a group of hunters coming up over the hill in pursuit of the deer. The herd got down to the highway, where there was a fence, and they started jumping over it. There was a doe who jumped, hit the top of the fence and fell back. One of the deer jumped back over the fence and stayed with her, and nudged her until she was able to jump the fence.

I want to ask a favor of you. When you finish this chapter, pray for our mother the earth and all of the creatures that she nurtures. Before you go to sleep, think of them. Think of our earth, think of her natural resources. Think about the things you are doing at home that may be harming her. Mother Nature has so much to give us. Think of her as you drift into sleep and be thankful. You will have forgotten the self.

The Center of the Wheel

Each of us will get out of life exactly what we put into it. We bring to life our agendas and motives and that is exactly what we get. We are always listening and looking for something in particular, and the paradox of that is that we often miss what is necessary. So let go, if you can. Empty yourself and allow yourself to be present. That is all you need to do. Just be present to this Dharma, incomparably profound and minutely subtle in its transmission, in its manifestation.

Two-and-a-half millennia ago, the Buddha asked, "What is the cause of suffering?" This is the quintessential question. The Four Noble Truths of Buddhism declare that life is suffering. This suffering is to be understood as a constant in life. Life is always suffering; even in the most pleasurable moments, suffering is present. This suffering is best understood by our attempt to grasp the moment in such a way that we want it to stay as it is. When we do this, we miss out on other opportunities for freedom. Life is suffering, whether we like to say it or not, whether we like to hear it or not.

I remember a friend of mine who worked in a cancer ward saying one day, "Yes, we don't like to see it, but suffering is everywhere." We tend to spend a great deal of our time averting our eyes from this reality because it's difficult to grasp. The problem with the Buddha Dharma or Zen practice for people is that its exclusive objective is to know the truth. That is to say, not my truth or some truth dictated by God or Buddha, but reality: To know it through and through; to know it in one's gut, in one's heart; to experience it; to become one with the eternal.

When the Buddha talked about suffering, he said that the cause of suffering is ignorance. Ignorance can be subtle. We do not always recognize it. I was watching a documentary the other day about a dysfunctional family in the Midwest which, as most stories of dysfunctional families do, had a tragic ending. The young son was convicted to half his life in jail because he had killed his mother. But the story was not about just that. It was also about the cause of the murder. What could possibly lead up to such a horrible incident in both a child's and a parent's life? One of the recurrent themes was that that the mother abused her children because of her ignorance and it went on to the point where this boy couldn't take it anymore. When the creators of the program discussed this ignorance, they came to the same conclusion that the Buddha came to 2500 years ago: that ignorance is the cause of untold sorrow. The boy's sister kept on saying that they didn't know that children were not supposed to be beaten by their mothers and the mother didn't know that she was not supposed to beat her children.

What is the cause of this suffering -- both the profound suffering in this story and the pervasive suffering that manifests itself in all life? The cause of it again and again turns on ignorance. The Buddha said that we do not know who we truly are, that we do not know what life is. And as any therapist will tell you, when we become trapped in ignorance and dysfunction we make choices and we live in ways that harm us. We live in relationships that are harmful and we make choices that do not serve our well-being. The Buddha wanted to understand this suffering deeply, intimately, and this is the purpose of our practice -- to become intimate with our lives as they are. Too often we take our lives for granted. WE TAKE OUR LIVES FOR GRANTED. We have no sense of responsibility for taking care of ourselves, let alone strangers or the planet or anything as abstract as that.

Buddhism calls us to an intimate relationship with life. Zen practice is the choice to engage life as a relationship, to know the truth about life through and through a means of becoming one with the eternal. In the Tao Te Ching, Lao Tzu says that one of the reasons why our life involves suffering has to do with our point of view. Buddha says that we focus our attention on those things that cause suffering. We focus our attention in the wrong direction. The Tao Te Ching also points to this. It says that we join spokes together in a wheel but it is the center hole that makes the wagon move. If we use the idea of a car as a metaphor, we could say that the outer layer of the tire is the first place most of us look when we feel our cars bouncing around.

When a mechanic checks your car, he doesn't necessarily look first at the tire; he looks at the wheel – the source of the motion. We can say that the rubber of the tires is our life's story, and that's where most of us are focused. That's when our point of view becomes skewed.

You don't need to look hard to see this. We each have a story to tell and that is where our attention always is. When our lives become difficult, we always go to the story. The story is the inventory of our lives: what we have, what we don't have; how we feel, how we don't feel; what we think, what we don't think; what we like, what we don't like. This is the rubber of the tire. This is the story of our lives. The Buddha said that we are always focused on that.

The way we try to fix life is to add things or to take things out of it, to get the right things into our lives, to possess as much as possible. The Buddha teaches us, the Tao teaches us, that this is the wrong focus. What makes the wheel turn is the emptiness at the center. We shape clay into a pot, but it is the emptiness inside that holds whatever we want. So again, our focus is always on what appears to be so evident to us. We need to become intimate with the space inside. The world we live in, the things we see around us, are manifestations of the inner state of being. We manifest outwardly what is going on inwardly. This is true about individuals, about societies, about politics -- about everything. The Tao Te Ching says our focus should be on that which holds what we want.

We hammer wood for a house, but it is the resulting interior that makes it livable. We can create things to be as perfect as we want. We can fill our houses with all kinds of pretty things, but it is the inner space that makes it livable. Maybe what we need to ask is whether we have enough livable space. Do we have the inner space? Are we open enough for the Dharma to live within us, to transform us? We have this wrong view that things do things to us. This is contrary to the Buddha Dharma. The Buddha Dharma teaches that when you are truly content within, when your foundation is truly solid, not even the fiercest tempests can move you. Jesus taught this to his disciples when he warned them about building their houses on sand. When the rains and the ocean waves come, no matter how beautiful the house may be, no matter how solid the oak, no matter the quality of the nails, no matter the expertise of the carpenter, the foundation will shift and the house will collapse.

The Tao points to the same thing: it is not the wood of the house, it is not the color of the house, it is not the material of the house -- it is the space within the house that determines whether or not it is livable. "We work with being." What is the Tao Te Ching saying here? That we have these bodies, we have these personalities, we have these false senses of self, and this is what we must work with in our practice. But non-being is what we use to achieve the objective of freedom, contentment and compassion.

To this end, Buddhism teaches that all beings possess the eternal qualities of love, compassion and wisdom. Theses are the three characteristics of that which we call the eternal. It is within us and everyone has the capacity to selflessly love other beings and to make a viable contribution to life. The Buddha says that we do not know this because we do not look for those things. Your mind and your daily living are always focused on the temporal. This will never bring contentment and is in fact the cause of suffering. We are constantly focused on our feelings. We are not drug addicts; we are feeling addicts. WE ARE ADDICTED TO OUR FEELINGS. Every day of our lives we are focused on how we feel, what we want, what we like, what we don't like; and we live out of our feelings. The Buddha Dharma invites us to understand that, "The planets that will outlive you and me, the trees and the mountains that will outlive you and me, the stars that will outlive you and me, the space that surrounds us is benignly indifferent to our complaints." That is to say that the eternal does not depend upon feelings, does not depend upon thought, and does not depend upon beliefs or desires. The eternal depends upon something that transcends of all of this. It is the objective of our practice to know this through and through and to become one with it. When the Buddha said that there is liberation from suffering, he was pointing to this. What is the cause of freedom? What liberates us from suffering? Knowing this truth experientially, knowing it through and through, becoming one with the eternal.

How so we do that? At the heart of Buddhist practice is zazen. No zazen, no Buddha Dharma. The Buddha taught seated meditation as an essential part of three jewels of liberation –the Buddha, dharma, and sangha. But if one meditates without having a principle in one's life or a purpose greater than one's self, then seated meditation is nothing more than just another self indulgence and it causes suffering. The Buddha talked about zazen as interconnected to the precepts, as the way of compassion, as the way of intimate engagement in the care of all the many beings. One cannot talk about the interconnectedness of zazen and the precepts without finally talking about the Sangha. The relationship that Buddhists share with all the many beings is not some subtle membership in a club. It is much more profound than that. It is the stewardship of life. It is people coming together, supporting and empowering each other to transcend those things in their lives that cause suffering, and to realize for themselves their own Buddha nature. These are the three characteristics of the liberated person: daily seated meditation; living the precepts; and a sense of responsibility for the planet, for people, for everything that exists. Liberation entails a sense of responsibility for me and the elimination of frivolity in my life. Frivolity tempts me to take time for granted, people for granted, to be consumed by busyness and the pursuit of things that don't last. It prevents me from hearing my inner voice. It keeps me from thinking about the quiet desperation that Henry David Thoreau describes as the quality of most men's lives.

The path to freedom demands of us that we be authentic, that we feel the truth. It means taking hold of one's life, cleaning it up, straightening it out, and then keeping it straight. This is what we mean by responsibility. Think about it. How often, except when you are feeling sick, do you really take care of yourself? You get up in the morning and you notice that it's mostly a routine. You've been doing it the same way for years. There's no real attention involved. We talk about our morning routine, our daily routine, our evening routine. The word "routine" is a really a code word for inattentive living.

We do not sit and meditate to escape that reality. We sit and meditate to become intimately aware of how we feel about our inattentive living. We do this because what we are ultimately headed for is an awareness of our follies. Here's an example of how I worked through one of my follies: I used to smoke when I was a teenager. There were no warning labels on the packages back then. I was up to three packs a day before I finally stopped smoking. People ask me how I stopped. Frankly, I think that I stopped the only way that you can stop. I got sick from it. I got sick of it. I had the flu and persisted in smoking. I was coughing and hacking so much that I just got sick of it. I never picked up another cigarette again. No patches, no doctors, nothing. I just got sick and tired of smoking.

Sometimes I think the spiritual life is the same way. When I look at Jesus' life, for example, it points to this. I tell Christians, that they all want to get into heaven without descending into hell. They all want the resurrection without the crucifixion. It didn't even work that way for God's own son! What makes you so special?

Zazen is the place where we become intimately aware of what it feels like to smoke with the flu. We sit in a certain way and in a certain posture and we look inside of ourselves. We feel our feelings without turning on the radio. How many of us turn on a radio so that we don't have to hear the still small voice within. We sit in these postures rather than getting in our cars and going to the malls.

Boredom is a message. When you are bored it means that there is something that you don't want to see about yourself. The Buddha was profoundly baffled by this. We are afraid of being alone with ourselves. We fill our lives with things and activities and goals. When people talk about goals to me, they're not talking about it in the way we talk about it in Zen. They're talking about a desperation to become something so that their lives will be secure and safe. In Zen, we talk about goals in terms of freedom and satisfaction and joy.

So when we sit and meditate, our objective is self study -- to become intimately aware of what is going on within us. The question then becomes, "Okay now I'm aware; I may not like it; it's not so comfortable; I don't want to hear anymore about this, so what do I do?" I come back to my story about quitting smoking. I never had a problem with wanting to smoke a cigarette again ever in my life. And I attribute that to the fact that I got so sick from smoking that I was just able to walk away from it. Zazen is just like that. You sit with all of your stuff, become totally aware of it, and do nothing with it. What we usually do with our stuff is to continually shuffle it around. Notice how you shuffle and rearrange the things in your house. We do the same thing internally. We can do this so quickly that we are not aware that we are doing it. During Zazen, there is no shuffling. When a thought comes up, allow it to come up and allow it to go. When a feeling comes up, allow it to come up and allow it to go.

When I sit in the zendo early in the morning, I like to have the window open no matter how cold it is outside because I like to hear the sounds of the animals. When I get settled into my seat, the first sound that I hear is the choir of crickets. I hear the sound of the crickets, but I don't think about it. I allow the sound of the crickets to appear, and I allow it to disappear. When the memory of a past experience shows up, I allow it to show up, but I don't think about it, all the while observing my mind, which I also call myself. Whenever you and I talk about ourselves, we are actually talking about these thoughts and feelings that are constantly flowing through us.

When we examine the mind long enough, we realize that it is nothing more than random, fluctuating thought. There is nothing metaphysical about it; it is nothing more than energy coming and going in the form of thoughts and feelings. We like to think that we are in control. One of the things that Zazen teaches us is that we are not in control.

One day not too long ago, I was doing zazen and listening to the crickets when I heard a cracking sound in the woods. All of a sudden, I was thinking about my grandmother, then I was thinking about what I had to do at work later, then I was singing the song from the Flintstones. This went on and on until finally I started to chuckle and I said, "THIS IS INSANITY." And I could hear the Buddha from 2500 years ago say, "YES IT IS." We have built our whole lives on insanity. You have these thoughts, you feel these feelings and you think it means something. Well, it doesn't.

The Buddha said thoughts come and go, feelings come and go, people come and go. The only things I can rely on as mine are my actions, what I choose to do. The problem we have with doing this returns to the cause of suffering, which is ignorance. When we do not know this intimately about the mind, we make choices and we create goals that are a function of serving madness and not eternity. We make choices out of fear rather than freedom. We make choices out of anger rather than love -- anger with ourselves or anger with others, it doesn't matter. And so the path to freedom must begin first with an awareness of the madness and ultimately, no matter how long it takes, to an awareness of our true nature, our Buddha nature.

Buddha nature is everywhere. It is in your meditation seats, it is in you, it is all around you, everywhere, but you do not see it because our minds are preoccupied by the madness of our thoughts and the feelings. We can say that zazen is the bridge from madness to the eternal. In the beginning, our zazen is noisy. Thoughts and feelings wrestle with each other -- thinking this way, feeling that way, up and down, side to side. As we continue to practice, things begin to settle down. When we understand that thoughts and feelings have no real power over us, they flow more easily. They stick around only if we cling to them. When thoughts appear during zazen and I indulge in thinking about them, it is like reaching out and grabbing them and holding them near. Don't think or as some teachers say, don't add another thought to that arising thought. The more I practice not adding to and holding onto thoughts, the more my interior becomes emptier and emptier until I reach the void, the beginningless silence, the silent sound of the eternal.

It is within this empty space, this quiet place, that anything can be held. Once you reach this silence; you will learn what is effective for living and what will bring contentment and joy and peace. It follows from this that you can fill that space with contentment and joy and love. You can't do this self consciously. The moment you think about love, it is not love. The moment you think about being compassionate, you can't be compassionate. The moment you try to be wise, you can't be wise. What you will find in the void IS compassion, IS love, IS wisdom. Actually, it's already there. Our task is to make our way through the welter of thoughts and feeling that run our lives in order to reach it.

49

Buddhist practice is the effective stripping away of that which crowds your life. If you try to get rid of these things, it will not work. That kind of self-conscious activity is fear driven. You may be tempted to call Charlie and say, "Get out of my life!" and you can go to your boss and say, "Take this job and shove it!" You can do fear-driven things like this. But "Charlie" will show up again. Even if you go and work for Greenpeace, that overbearing boss will eventually appear in another person. It's not "Charlie." It's not your nasty boss. It's what's going on within you.

The world becomes transformed in the same way as when a young man falls in love. Suddenly that difficult world in which he finds himself becomes beautiful everywhere he goes. The Buddha Dharma teaches that we can know love, be in love and experience love regularly if we know how. But the way we have been doing it up until now will not work. And so the first step is to change the way we live and to see the interconnectedness of the Buddhist precepts with the practice of zazen.

We can talk about the Buddhist precepts individually. We can talk about not killing and not gossiping and not stealing and all of that, but I'd rather address the spirit of the precepts. The spirit of the precepts is defined this way: From now on, my life is not just about my life. From now on I am the caretaker of life. All life now becomes my life. All the many beings now become me. The precepts are a way of describing love. If love is not loving, it is not love. If love is not caring for another, is not taking care of something more than just myself, then it's worthless. So, again, I sit not to feel better, even though I will eventually; I sit not to be happier, even though I will eventually; I sit to become intimately aware of my interconnectedness with all life. Through the living of the precepts I practice active meditation. The precepts are another form of meditation. When I meditate, I will get out of it exactly what I bring to it. So if I bring to my meditation anything other than what I have just described to you, it won't work. In the same way, if it is my sincere intention to know all the many beings intimately, I will know them. As Jesus taught his disciples, it is in loving your neighbor that you love yourself. The experience of love becomes available to me only when I love someone else. I experience love not because of something someone has done for me.

The interconnectedness of zazen, the precepts, and a deliberate engagement with other beings on the Buddha path are the formulas for freedom prescribed by the Buddha. Sangha is the testing ground for living in the world in this way. It's easy to love the world in general, but the real evidence of our love is in the way we treat the person right next to us. This love extends to other beings as well. In Zen we handle everything with reverence. We handle the spiders in our bedrooms with reverence. If you do this long enough, you then develop a fascination for other creatures. They become your friends.

The other day I was working outside when I saw a salamander on the door. I called one of the monks over to look at it. She picked it up carefully and we were able to look at it long enough to see how beautiful it was. And then we let it go. Suddenly we saw the beauty in everything. Everything is engaging when you take the time to look at it. For instance, I've never liked spiders. I even came to hate them at one point in my life. So here I am today, living in a monastery where they are everywhere. And not just little spiders, but big suckers! I open up a window and there one of them is, staring right at me as if to say, "When are we going to be friends?" It's interesting how karma is. What you resist in your life will persist until you become friends with it. That's how life is. You cannot run away from your life. You may think you can, but you can't. The purpose of your life is to handle it. If you don't do it now, you'll come back again and again until you do. The spiders will continue to crawl all over you and bite you until you discover that there is another way of being with spiders and they become your friends, your brothers, your sisters.

A popular story that often comes up among Tibetans concerns an English engineer who came to Tibet to work on a dam. There were 100,000 Tibetans involved. All of a sudden at one end of the dam the operation stopped and nobody would work. Evidently, they had found a spider while they were working and proceeded to create a little pile of dirt for the spider so that it would not get hurt. Nobody would proceed with the work until they got that little spider out of the way. The engineer was dumbfounded. That spider was family. Life becomes a wonderful place where you are never alone; your family is everywhere you go. In this way, there is no more loneliness, no desperation, no searching for someone. You find them right in front of you and all around you. But you've got to know how to do it.

Zazen, having a purpose in your life by which you live with integrity, and Sangha, are the three vehicles that lead to freedom. All are interconnected. You can't have one without the other in order for spiritual unfolding to work. You can't sit and meditate without keeping the precepts and without being involved in a community of like-minded people. We do not walk this path alone and you are responsible for everyone else. *Jesus also*

The Buddha Dharma tells us that we must turn around. Wrong view means that we are looking in the wrong direction. We need to be looking within ourselves and we need to be doing the work of creating both external and internal silence. You can move into our monastery and you will find that, if you don't have the radio or the TV on, it is very peaceful. Visitors pay lip service to our peaceful surroundings but it runs thin for them after a while. They can't take it for very long. Internal peace is even more difficult to cultivate. If we don't have that, we get bored and uncomfortable with external peace and we have to distract ourselves with something. The trick is in balancing internal and external peace. Practice is in learning internal peace so as to cultivate external peace. Practice is also cultivating internal compassion, to begin feeling compassion within for all the many beings, to feel compassion everywhere. Our practice is to be in relationship so that we will see it everywhere we go. We practice being with nonbeing. What is that? Nonbeing refers to not bringing our stuff into the moment. As with zazen, we live each moment the same way. We live each moment as it is and do our part to contribute to its benefit, not to get it to be as we want it to be.

Can you coax your mind from its wandering and keep to the original oneness? Can you let your body become as supple as a newborn child's? Can you cleanse you inner vision until you see nothing but the light? Can you love people and lead them without imposing your will? Can you deal with the most vital matters by letting events take their course? Can you step back from your own mind and thus understand all things? Giving birth and nourishing, having without possessing, acting with no expectations, leading and not trying to control, this is the supreme virtue.

We often think that spiritual life is a kind of supplement to the way we are living. For example, we usually do things with expectations. We expect that life will give us something back if we do certain things. We expect that people will love us back a certain way if we love them. The way of the eternal is to love without expectations -- to be forgiving without expectations; to be compassionate without expectations; to practice Zen without expectations; to keep the precepts without expectations. In Soto Zen, the practice of zazen and enlightenment is the same thing. We are to understand that we do not practice zazen to become enlightened. When we practice zazen, when we keep the precepts, we are enlightened. When we do not practice zazen, when we do not live the precepts, suffering arises.

Can you sit with your thoughts and feelings and allow them to come and go? Can you devote yourself to a goal without any personal agenda? Can you care for another person without any expectations? Can you become, as his Holiness the Dalai Lama would ask, the servant of all servants? If not, you have a longer journey than you think. The very things that we have spent our lives averting, will be the very instruments of our freedom. Everything is practice. I say this and it gets misconstrued into all sorts of things I never intended. What I want you to understand when I say this is that the very issues that you have not overcome yet in your life are your practice. Do you want to know what you have to do with your life in order to get it to the place of the eternal? Look at the things you keep doing that cause you and others to suffer. THAT is your practice. Zazen makes us intimately aware of our issues, and the Sangha certainly makes us intimately aware of them. Each day we need to create the intention to look at our issues. What am I doing that keeps causing the same painful result? Whatever that is, DON'T DO IT. There are things I do in my life that benefit myself and others. Whatever it is, I DO IT. Others and I are the same. When my practice becomes something I do for myself alone, I've missed the point. We need each other for our freedom. Therefore no one is ever really free until all beings are free.

When you wake up in the morning, make a vow: However innumerable all beings are, I vow to love each and very one of them. Now, does God or anyone else expect that you will be capable of doing that? No. So lighten up! But you vow it anyway and you work on it. And when you work on it long enough you will keep it. However inexhaustible my desires are in the course of the day, I vow to extinguish them all. However immeasurable the Dharma is, I vow to master it. Never, never go a day or a moment outside the role of a student. The Dharma is incomparably profound; there are lessons everywhere. Study them. Look at life. When was the last time you really looked at life, really stopped to smell a rose and become aware of its essence? Look at that salamander. Look at the people in front of you before you judge them. Look at them. However endless this way of living may be, for however long it takes me, I promise I will follow it.

These are the vows of a free person. To endlessly vow to follow the Way no matter how difficult, no matter how taxing, no matter how long it takes, is like saying that no matter what you do, you can be sure that I love you. If you choose to go in one direction, I will love you. If you choose to go in another direction, I will love you. That is what we all hunger for from others.

I am utterly convinced that the way in which a person becomes self-confident is through self-discipline. If I break my vows too often, then I will never know my unlimited potential. The only reason that I don't get to the top of the mountain is that I keep quitting half way. That is the only reason -- not because the mountain is tough, but because I keep quitting halfway. I keep quitting because I haven't effectively learned how to practice the Dharma; I haven't learned how to climb to the top of the mountain.

Effective living acknowledges these endless vows. If we bring this to our practice of the Dharma, then we will know eternity.

I have been practicing this way for thirty-some years now and there is never a time in which my practice does not require refinement. We too often make the error that we've gotten to a point where we have learned everything. I have found that to be the biggest falsehood of our lives. Even Zen masters are always learning and learning and learning. One of the things that I am always refining is my practice of zazen. Even those of you who have been students for a long time fall into the trap of assuming that zazen is just about getting into the postures and going through the motions when the bell rings.

I find this not to be true. For example, when I wake up early in the morning for our dawn sitting, my thoughts and feelings are churning before I enter the Zendo. When this happens, there is something I need to do. When I take my seat, I must calm myself in order to begin the meditation. In this way, zazen becomes a way of taking hold of your life. We must recognize that there is this continuous, automatic thinking and feeling within each of us. The mind does not need you to think and feel. During the course of the day you know that your feelings change randomly. I don't think there is any one who has not had the experience of having a pleasant day and then all of a sudden feeling sad. We get trapped into trying to do something about that reaction because we do not understand the nature of what is going on.

What is going on is that the mind is a thinking machine. It is information in motion. Zazen is the means by which we take charge of this. That means doing the things that I need to be doing in order to be a whole person from moment to moment. To this end, what we miss often is the Buddhist teaching that you and I are already complete. We are already complete. We do not sit zazen to become Buddha's; we sit zazen because we are Buddha's. We don't live the Dharma to be better people; we live the Dharma because we are better people than we think we are. We have the capacity to be vibrantly alive. But what we have done is to suppress our knowledge of this and push it out of our lives. Have you ever noticed how when love shows up it is a fantastic event for us? The reason why we don't see it all the time is because we are not living lives that allow us to see it all the time.

When I do zazen, I am saying that I am going to take charge of my life. I may not be able to do it consistently at work; I may not be able to do it consistently when I am driving down the expressway; I may not be able to do it while I am busy taking care of the children; but when I sit, I am saying that for this moment I am going to take charge of my life. As monks, we do this in the morning and at night. When I wake up in the morning, the day is already starting to take control of me. My thoughts are already churning. Here it is, four in the morning, but my mind has jumped to nine in the morning and the work ahead. What I have to do is stop all of this before I sit. I take a deep breath, and I demand silence. Sometime I even say it. "Silence." And then I sit. This is how I begin my zazen.

I am convinced that without reverence, practices such as zazen are not possible. I am convinced about this no matter what the tradition is -- Buddhist, Christian, Jewish, Muslim, Hindu. Buddhist gassho and bow. When we do this long enough, we understand the brevity of life. I remember sitting with my Catholic friend talking about the sacredness of life and he asked me why I thought that life is sacred. I replied that it's so delicately present and then it is gone. The more you cultivate the silence of zazen, the more you learn how to touch something and hold it and keep in mind not only its impermanence, but your own. This becomes very real. It's not just a Buddhist thing or a Catholic thing.

Every moment is sacred. We bow to it. We do this during zazen as an expression of gratitude. If you practice long enough you will experience this. Zazen becomes something different from what Zen students say it is. It is no longer an obligatory act. It becomes a gift, an opportunity to stop and experience the gift of life. I often think about the day when I will no longer have this opportunity, when I will no longer be able to smell the beauty of firewood, of incense, of blue skies, when I will no longer be able to gaze upon the beauty of the zendo. When I contemplate all of this, it becomes clear to me that life is a gift.

On the Pathway

Living with the Truth of Suffering

What is practice as we refer to it? What is Zen practice? As I mentioned earlier, the Buddha said there are four noble facts about existence, about the universe, about life. When one has penetrated these facts in such a way that one has truly come face to face with them and understood them through and through, not just with the intellect, then one will achieve the most important purpose of life, which is to awaken to life as it is. The First Noble Truth about suffering is like a giant wall to overcome.

To be alive, to exist, means suffering. Get beyond it. Get over it. There is physical suffering, there is emotional suffering, and there is the psychological suffering involved with existence. Humans suffer, animals suffer, trees suffer, grass suffers, all life suffers. Until I embrace this fact of life, there is no possibility that the other three remaining Noble Truths will make sense. Life is suffering. That is the nature of all existing matter. The moment something is born, its death is implied. We don't like to think about this, yet if we do not open our eyes to the truth of our own existence, we are living in a dream.

We are not going to get around the Second Noble Truth and the fact that our bodies are temporal and do not last; the decay and the illness that leads to death are inevitable. The Buddha was clear that we have a choice in dealing with suffering. There is a cause for it. Suffering arises from ignorance. That is to say, sometime in my life, I disconnected with it and identified with something else. You can imagine it this way: suddenly there appears in your existence a "self." Now, this self is the self that I call myself. From that moment forward, I begin to create my world from the point of view of this self. We refer to this point of view as perception. That is to say, this self begins to perceive the world in a particular way. Even when there are similarities in the perceptions of different people, there will still be differences upon which we can flounder. When that happens, there will be suffering.

In the Third Noble Truth, the Buddha said that there is hope. There is cessation from that form of suffering. One can rise above mental, emotional and psychological suffering. One can also rise above physical suffering to a certain degree. The cessation of suffering is described as a way of living. This way of living is described for us in the Fourth Noble Truth. It is called the Eightfold Noble Path, and it is called a path for a reason. When one comes upon a fork in a road, one has two choices. As Robert Frost said, "Two roads diverged into the woods and I took the one less traveled by." One can either choose to walk the path or not walk the path. It is called the path because it must be traveled, or more accurately, it must be lived, practiced, put into one's daily living.

At a very early age, when I disconnected from life, from being truly alive, I fell asleep. When I fell asleep into this dream-state world that I call "myself," I found that suffering has been ever present. When I look at the world, I see suffering. When I am willing to be honest about my experience, there is suffering. It takes many different forms: I don't know what I want to do with my life; I should do it this way; I should do it that way. It takes the form of committing to something and not following through with one's commitments. It takes the form of not saying what one really means or of not meaning what one says. Suffering also takes the more profound forms of expressing anger in a way that hurts others, that takes others for granted. It assumes subtle forms: depression, not knowing, confusion, and worry about the future. It affects relationships, as in dishonesty about what one really wants from them. The forms of slavery, both emotional and physical, are manifestations of suffering. We learn to become content with our discontentment. Thoreau spoke about the quiet desperation of our lives. I've found that it is not really so silent when you take the time to listen.

The Buddha understood that suffering was a fact of human existence. No human being, including the Buddha, has come into life without forgetting who he or she truly is and falling asleep into a dream world. In the world of discontentment, in the world of attachment to this self that I call myself, my actions take the form of always being concerned about satisfying myself. As Eihei Dogen said, when I begin to study the self, I find out that the reality is that even though I have disguised it at times, I am always thinking about me:

how I feel, what I want, what I like, what I don't like. Even when I think I am complaining about injustice in the world, when I look closely at it, what I am talking about is my own discontent. This self I call myself is sly and very keen.

All of this points to the same issue: the practice of liberation is work. It is difficult work. Not because it is the nature of the practice itself, but because we have learned to be content with our discontentment. And the only time we seem to be anywhere near wanting to do anything about it is when we are uncomfortable. And this is where the paradox lies. The Zen masters of ancient times would say to you that if you do anything about your discomfort, it is the same thing, it is still self-serving. It is no different from saying, "I'm too hot. I'll turn on the air-conditioning." So what is real practice?

Zazen is a deliberate effort to wake up and pay attention to the moment. It is not passively sitting around waiting for enlightenment to pop up. It never happens that way. It does not come by surprise. The individual who has awakened to his or her own enlightenment met a prerequisite before that moment. What was that? When we read the story of Dogen's own enlightenment, some of us mistakenly believe that it was by some kind of grace or miracle that he observed a cook and awakened to life. For proper understanding, one must look at what Dogen brought to that moment while observing the cook -- his full attention to someone else other than himself. What is that? What is it to be fully attentive to something or someone else other than myself? Possibly it was out of that moment that Dogen went on to define Zen by saying that Zen is the study of the self.

Understanding the anatomy of the self begins by becoming aware of the little self that runs our day-to-day lives. Many students never get that far. They never take responsibility for their lives to the point where they stop blaming external factors for their experiences and embrace the fact that this self I call myself is shaping my experience of the world around me, for me, at all times.

Dogen went on to say that in order to thoroughly study the self we must forget the self. We must forget our self in order to thoroughly appreciate its power in our lives. The next time you want something, give up wanting it. Whatever it is, just don't act on wanting it. Maybe it's sleeping a little bit longer. Maybe it's food. Maybe it's drink. Maybe it's some possession. Maybe it's some supposedly gratifying place to live. Watch what happens. Watch it; notice it. It is the self at work. Don't act on it. Conversely, whatever frightens you, do it. Don't run away from it; don't try to find a way out of it. Watch this little self suffer. The next time someone asks you, "What do you think about this?" see how it is your practice to be dishonest, which is acceptable in our society. Instead, tell him or her exactly what you think. Watch yourself and see how you feel. The next time you have a criticism or opinion, keep it to yourself. Watch that obnoxious individual get praise and glory while you could step in to stop it. Keep it to yourself and watch what happens.

To study the self is to become aware of its presence in your day-to-day choices. "What is running you? What is the driving force in your life?" Twenty-five hundred years ago, when the Buddha set out to answer this he stopped playing at life. He chose to really look into himself. One could say that he finally prepared himself to be alive. But he saw that to really be alive, to really be in the world, he had to step out of it. That is what going to a Zen monastery is about. That is what your daily zazen is all about -- stepping out of the world. While you are sitting Zen, for example, you are doing the same thing you do throughout the day. Nothing has changed and nothing will change. When we come to Zen practice, we choose to leave the supposed security of a particular life style. To study the self is to look at it. This self I call myself is not the bad guy, it is a powerful teacher and an instrument for liberation. But if I am not engaged in watching it and learning about its presence in my day-to-day choices, then I cannot progress in my practice. Whatever else you learn, even if you read about it, even if you listen to Roshis talk about it, you will learn nothing unless you apply it moment by moment in your life. The Buddha had nothing to offer beyond this. When a Japanese master would go up to the altar and throw a Buddha statue into the fire, he was trying to tell his students that Buddhism has no value if you do not put it into practice. The practice is stepping out of our business.

One of the ways in which the self disguises itself is to make our life busy. We convince ourselves that we are ruled by time and commitments. That is a lie. It is a lie that you and I created. We learned it from our mothers and fathers in order to avoid what is necessary. What is necessary here and now is to be present to here and now. When someone calls us on the telephone and we say to them, "Listen, can I get back to you? I don't really have the time to talk to you now," that is part of the lie. When you decide that you don't have time to pay attention to the moment, to go and sit, to listen to the person who is talking to you, you are lying to yourself and to them and to the moment. Time is an illusion. It doesn't really exist. It was created by the self to manage itself. Time did not exist until human beings said, "Let's create time, let's give it a beginning, a middle, and an end." It does not exist. There is no such thing as twenty-four hours in a day. There is no such thing as today there is no such thing as tomorrow; it is a manufactured perception of reality. So when I talk about not having enough time, I am lying. I am deceiving myself and I am deceiving others.

We will never learn what it is to be truly fully alive and free until we overcome our perceived limitations, and that is what practice is about. Practice is about deliberately working to overcome this self and all of its little, little complaints about life. It is as if complaining loudly enough and long enough will change the fact that suffering is a part of life. The Buddha said, "Life is suffering. Get over it."

The Buddha wanted us to understand that the path to Nirvana is in learning to live with life as it is. Most of us do not effectively live with life as it is. As Mother Theresa said, we cannot help the poor by talking about the poor. We cannot end poverty by thinking about poverty. We help the poor by helping the poor. We end poverty by ending poverty. In other words, "Just do it." Jesus teaches us that when your brother is hungry, give him some of your bread. When your sister is thirsty give her some of your drink. When people are naked in the streets, give them some of your clothing. Just do it. It doesn't matter if you are rich or poor, it doesn't matter if you live in a hermitage in the mountains, it doesn't matter if you live in the city, it doesn't matter if you are a Buddha and it doesn't matter if you are a sentient being. Life is suffering, and an enlightened being knows it.

When one begins to study the self, one begins to look at the causes of suffering. The chief cause of suffering is that we would rather think about life than live it. This is what the Buddha realized about himself. While he was thinking about his life, while he was thinking about the world and how it was, a lot of suffering was going on. But when he deliberately engaged it face to face, and learned how to live it and experience it as it was there was no suffering. No suffering. Simple.

One of my first childhood experiences of seeing someone just being present happened on a day when I was having lunch at a friend's house. My friend's oldest brother was a very quiet fellow. He was also very gentle. He played basketball like no one else did, but was not haughty about his abilities. He and I and my friend were sitting around the table when one of the neighbors came running in. She was hysterical because her little brother had fallen down the front steps and gone right through a pane glass window. It had sliced his arm open and he was bleeding profusely. My friend's older brother got up and grabbed a towel from the sink. He ran to the house with us close behind him. When we got there, he grabbed the boy, laid him down, wrapped the towel around his arm and said, "Call the ambulance." He simply acted with no deliberation. That impressed me for the rest of my life.

How was it he knew what to do without thinking about it? How was it that he was able to just act and save the boy from bleeding to death? No emotion was involved, no panic was involved. There was none of that. While he was doing this, you need to know that others were frantically running around saying, "What should we do? Where is this? Where is that?" He was already at the boy's side. He was already there, in action, saving the little boy's life.

When we talk about being present, it's like that. Just do what needs to be done in the moment, here and now. If you waste time thinking, you are squandering time and killing life. If you are not capable, then you need to become capable. If my friend's brother did not already have the disciplined ability to act, the outcome would have been different. We must learn how to live effectively. This takes discipline. This is what practice is. This is what are you doing as a Zen student, disciplining yourself to be present to life. There is no tomorrow to think about. When I ask, "Are you going to do what you need to do to be a Zen student?" I watch you go into your head and try to come up with the right answer. When I ask the question, I am not suffering. There is a lot of suffering in the answer that you give. "Well I don't know. I have a lot to do, and I don't know what tomorrow will bring, and I got this and I got that." There is the suffering that the Buddha spoke about. There it is -- all the confusion, all the questioning. By the time you get done, I would have bled to death.

The Cost of Ignorance

The ignorance that the Buddha spoke about refers to the fact that we do not know what the meaning, the purpose, of life is. We have disconnected from it and entered an illusory world called "myself." We have dedicated our lives to making <u>ourselves</u> feel good, to making <u>ourselves</u> happy, as if that were the purpose of life, as if that will bring us satisfaction. A life that is just about satisfying ourselves is never fulfilling. It doesn't work because its objective has nothing to do with the purpose, the meaning of existence.

If we do not become honest, if we do not tell the truth about what is wrong with our lives, then there is no possibility for evolving. But in order to be truthful, you must understand what Dogen meant when he said, "Zen is the study of the self." He meant that if you do not live with a moment by moment awareness of what your mind is doing, then there is no possibility for awakening; there is no possibility for change. The path to enlightenment begins with a deliberate effort to look into life, to look into how we live. It has nothing to do with some mystical, magical event that will take place when God comes around to liking me or the Buddha comes back and touches me with something. It begins and it ends with you right here, right now. It begins with your sitting with your discomfort. How many times have you sat Zen, shifted around in your seat, gotten another cushion, moved into a chair, and found it to be comfortable …until it wasn't. Why doesn't that work?

Because life is suffering. The Buddha way is to learn how to live effectively with it. Is it possible that you can be uncomfortable and still be true to yourself and to practice? For example, you are probably doing battle with the illusion that practice is in opposition to everything that you have to do. This habit of mind didn't start when you decided to study Zen. You've been doing it all your life. You have always been setting up one thing against something else.

You are always setting up time against being present in the moment or what is required to be present in the moment against time. The self is always viewing everything outside itself as being oppositional to it. Its only interest is in itself. We create perceived limitations. The self will tell you that it doesn't have time; it will tell you that practice is too difficult. It will tell you that you will never learn Zen. It will tell you that you will never achieve your own enlightenment. It will tell you it takes a lifetime so just sit back and wait for it to happen. The self is illusory because its purpose is not conducive to your freedom. This self I call myself is nothing more than a collection of thoughts and feelings that has separated me from my true nature and made me believe that it is who I am. It runs my life.

Zen sutras, like the ancient Christian and Judaic mystical writings, use such metaphors and allegories as going home, turning around, going back, finding oneself, finding one's true self. It is as if we have lost ourselves. But that is a metaphor too and nothing else, because it is not true on a deep level. What is true is that you have forgotten your true self and replaced it with the illusion of feelings and thoughts. I will live in this dream state until I learn how to effectively correct it and then effectively apply that awareness moment to moment, and deliberately discipline and devote myself to that practice.

Again, on a deep level nothing will change. I must choose to either do things the way that I always have done them – which causes suffering -- or to apply the awareness and understanding necessary to choose a new way out of suffering. The only way that I can do this is to recognize the results of my actions. In the thirty or so years that I have deliberately spent examining myself, I have come to learn that there are certain actions and ways of being that result in suffering. You will notice when you do this study that conditioned actions are easy. It doesn't take any effort to continue doing them. Over time, you will notice that there are other ways of doing and being that have different and more healthful consequences than do our conditioned responses to life.

The Buddha said, "Go and test this." So I tested it. There are methods that have proven time and again to result in fulfillment, satisfaction, and joy, despite difficulties. You will begin to notice that these practices can be difficult and that they may entail a bit of worry and fear. But there's also a sense that the practice will work. But I must pay attention and use the tools that I have learned. Part of the problem is that most of you don't even know what we need in order to be human. You haven't studied yourselves long enough to figure out that people must love others. People are designed to be lovers. The most fulfilling and contented times in my life are when I am genuinely caring for beings other than myself.

There is a wonderful story in Natalie Goldberg's book <u>Long Quiet Highway</u> about a flower that Dainin Katagiri Roshi had in the Minneapolis Zen Meditation Center. It was given to him long before she came to Minnesota. It was a beautiful flower that had lived much longer than flowers generally do. One day, Natalie was admiring this flower. She turned to Katigiri Roshi and she said, "Roshi, this flower is so beautiful!" And he said to her, "Yes Natalie, this is what happens when you take care of something." Zen is the practice of taking care of your life. We do not take care of our lives just for a sense of gratification. We nurture our lives in part for the sake of loving kindness.

For example, when we got Lotus, Aubrey, and Gabriel (three dogs that live at the monastery) we asked questions. What do these breeds require? What do these puppies require? We didn't just take the puppies' home and try to figure out what they needed. You see? That is what a lot of human beings do with their pets, don't they? They feed them food they should not be eating because they think, "Well, all they need is food." We do this to ourselves. We eat the wrong foods. We eat foods that cause illness, that cause disease, that cause cancer, and then we get angry about getting sick. The reason why we get angry is that the self deludes us into believing that something other than us is the cause of our suffering. Certainly, we think, it has nothing to do with the fact that I don't take care of my body, that I don't take care of my mind, that I don't take care of my environment, that I don't do the things that human beings need to be doing in order to live effectively, in order to be fulfilled in order to be satisfied.

When one comes to this practice, one must be prepared to make the deliberate decision to change that attitude quickly or nothing will change. Zen involves is practice. The way you have practiced up until this moment is not conducive to waking up. That is why we have teachers. A teacher must be involved, because he or she must be prepared to say to the student, "No, you don't understand; the way you've been doing it isn't going to work." It isn't going to work here.

Some people are in awe of my father, his energy, his discipline, and work ethic. Some people say, "I hope I am just like him when I am seventy-two years old!" Of course, he did not just become that way. What he is now is the sum of what he has done in the past. The future is right here in this moment. We are creating it right now. How I will be when I am seventy-two years old is determined, has been determined, and will continue to be determined, by what I do up until the time I reach his age.

A Question of Priorities

The story of the Buddha is our story. Only the details are different. He was a prince. He lived in a castle. He had a lot of money. This is certainly not our story, but in a way it is. You and I go through life believing that it's all about the things in our lives. We arrive at a place where we convince ourselves that life is all about acquiring "stuff." But it's not about the castle, the money and the new car. The Buddha realized that he had everything, yet he still felt discontentment and lack. The story about his hearing the women singing on the other side of the palace wall was a metaphor. Something about the sound, something about the quietness, something about the serenity in her voice, calmed the anguished chatter and unease in his mind. Yet even with this beautiful moment, he realized that he was not able to just enjoy the sound of her voice. There was still discontent. That motivated him. That is what caused him to leave on his spiritual quest. He recognized something about himself when he finally told the truth, "Even with all of this I am not content." Why? It is not the things in my life that will make me contented. It is not the people in my life that will make me contented. What will make me contented is how I live my life. What I am talking about is limited to me. What is that? My experience. No one's experience can cross over into another's, no matter what. Therefore I am the beginning and the end of my life's experience. I am causing it. I am creating it. I am both the actor and the director. This is not a philosophy.

Very Important.

I am the only person who can experience my life. No one can reach into that experience and know it as I know it. Why do we continue to rely on externals to make the changes we hunger for? The Buddha put it simply: We are ignorant. We do not understand that only we can make the changes in our lives; no Roshi can do it for us; no guru can do it for us, no Messiah can do it for us. Jesus came a little over 2,000 years ago as God Himself, and very little has changed. Are we to blame God for failing at His job? No. He was as clear about it as the Buddha was. The Good News has no value to you unless you live it. Love your neighbor. Oh how nice, what a beautiful thought. How many times have you said, "Oh what the world would be like if everybody did that?" Thinking about love doesn't change the world, but acting on it will. How many of you have thought how wonderful it would be if you could get through a sitting without too much struggle. This is the same type of question. Thinking about it will achieve nothing. It takes deliberate, decisive, disciplined effort. I don't literally mean for you to sit still and don't move. I mean learning how to sit in a way that works for you.

Each of us has our own seat. That is why you don't sit in my seat and I don't sit in your seat. Find your own seat. Finding your seat doesn't mean finding the right cushion or finding the right chair or finding the right location. An example of this makes the point. If an athlete has a game on Saturday night, where he is expected to win, and on Monday through Friday he drinks and eats what he shouldn't, doesn't exercise, and doesn't prepare himself for the game he won't amount to anything. Saturday night won't mean a thing. What he does at that game on Saturday night does not happen on Saturday night: It happens during the week before Saturday night. More accurately, his entire life before Saturday night brings about what happens on Saturday night.

Paul of Tarsus described the spiritual path just like the athlete's path. The athlete must know his body. The athlete must understand the way to eat, the way to drink, the way to sleep, the way to train the body, the way to live. The coach doesn't care when the athlete says, "Coach, I will not be at practice today because I don't have the time to come." The coach says, "You're fired." You don't get to play; you'll sit on the bench. Why does the coach put the athlete on the bench? Because for all practical purposes that's where he is already. Because the bench is where people just think about the game; they are not the players. The bench is where people talk about the game. The bench is where people know how to win the game. The crowd knows exactly what that athlete should have done to win the game. But if you were to pick one of them up out of the stands and put him in the game, it would be a disaster. The Buddha realized that in order to do this he would have to leave everything, until he achieved it. That's how much effort it took. Typically, when I get to this point in my talks most people are trembling in their seats or they are trying to figure out how they can do this and still keep everything they've got.

When God called Abraham to sacrifice his son, he didn't ask him to make a date. He didn't tell him to look at his calendar and get back to Him as to a convenient time to carry the kid up the mountain and kill his butt. God didn't ask him to do that. Abraham said, "Lord, thy will be done. What do I need to do?" Most people probably don't realize the tremendous difficulty Abraham must have had when God told him to do this. Cecil B. DeMill would have us believe that he just went up the mountain and did it. If any of you are parents, imagine being told that you have to kill your child in order to enter heaven and know God. That's what he was told.

Imagine Moses being told that, no matter what he did, he could not enter the Promised Land. God didn't reveal this at the end of the journey. God let him know about half way through the desert that he could get the people to the Promised Land but that he himself would never cross the Jordan River. Do you think that maybe Moses considered the possibly of telling God to screw Himself, that the people could wander for another 40,000 years as far as he was concerned? I bet you he did. I know I would have. What about Jesus? Where are you, God? Why are you leaving me here on this cross? And the Buddha. Do you think that if the Buddha tried to enlighten himself from within the walls of his palace that he would have been able to achieve it? Absolutely not. Why do we think it should be different for us? Are we just arrogant? I don't think that that's all there is to it. I think we really need to first recognize how we have become, as Natalie Goldberg says, "contented with our discontentment." We are lazy.

When I look at our culture today, I really hope to God there isn't another Pearl Harbor. I really hope there isn't. I pray each day for no natural disaster, even though it is probably what we need to wake up. We would really not know what to do. Look at what happens when people's computers go down. I was in the Reading Market in Philadelphia one day when the electricity failed. I wanted to buy something from an Amish farmer. I suggested that he take the money and use the surplus for his church. He said, "No, I have to weigh it first. The electricity is down and I have no way of doing it." I said to him, "What did your great grandfather do? He didn't have a computer." He said, "Oh, you just have to wait." We need to see the lesson in this and not just be entertained by it. This is your story. This is my story.

How many times do we imagine limitations as to why we can't do something? Our limitations are our own. Our excuses are our own. Our reasons are our own. They are not part of the universe. There's a wonderful line from Jurassic Park: "Life always finds a way." Life always finds a way, so why don't you? I think it has to do with fundamentals. This is not rocket science. You don't have to work hard at figuring this out. People are impressed with the fact that my father is seventy-two years old and still works the same hours he did when he was seventeen years old. He still has the same energy. He still has the same commitment. He still gets up at the same hour of the day. He still works the same hours, seven days a week. But he has trained and disciplined himself.

When we indulge our excuses, we become weak; we become lazy; we become disinterested. Laziness is like a drug. I don't want you to hear this as blame. I want you to see laziness as an instrument for practice. You must get beyond your laziness. Laziness is an obstacle to enlightenment. It is an obstacle to relationships. It is an obstacle to satisfaction. It is an obstacle to fulfillment. Laziness will oppose your ever being contented. We need to get beyond laziness. A person's excuse is equal to his or her word. Do not trust anyone who keeps coming up with excuses for not doing something. Get out of that relationship. Get out of it now. Get out.

We have to stop being a people of excuses and start being a people of our word. In addition, be very, very careful when our actions are all about pleasure and comfort. No one likes pleasure and comfort more than I do, but not too much of it. Balance is necessary. And the problem with us is that we've been trained to believe that comfort and pleasure is the prize. It is a poison. Snake handlers deal with poison all the time. But they know how to handle it. They don't listen to people who say, "Stop being a snake handler you fool. You'll be poisoned." That is not an alternative for a snake handler; it's not an option. If you want to be a snake handler, you have one of two choices. You get bitten and die or you learn how to handle them. That's what practice is. Life will kill you because you do not exist for life; life doesn't care about you. As a philosopher once wrote, "I experienced my own liberation when I realized the benign indifference of the planets and the stars to my complaints." God doesn't care. He didn't even listen to His own Son. So the snake handler has to learn how to handle difficult situations in order to be an effective snake handler, but more than that in order to stay alive. You must approach your practice in the same way. You must learn how to do it and then you must apply what you have learned every day. If you do, things will change, if you don't, things will not change.

The Paramitas: Walking the Pathway Skillfully

Freedom from Fearfulness

One of the major ways of cultivating a Buddhist sensibility is by refining the paramitas – the perfections of practice. There are six paramitas: generosity, ethics, patience, virtuous effort, meditative concentration, and transcendent wisdom. As you will see, these perfect practices are general enough to apply to essentially any spiritual discipline. The chapters that follow discuss our daily efforts to practice these paramitas in the situation that commonly confront us.

Imagine a very poor man living in a shanty, the only thing he owns in the world. What he does not know is that just beneath his shanty, but hidden in the dirt, is an inexhaustible vein of gold. As long as he remains ignorant of his hidden wealth, the pauper remains in poverty. But when he attends more closely to his own dwelling, he is bound to discover his own fathomless wealth. Similarly, all we need to do is unveil our own nature and we will find an inexhaustible source of wisdom, compassion and power. It is nothing we need to acquire from anywhere or anything. It has always been there. Seen in this light, the Buddha nature requires no additions, one does not have to memorize Sutras, recite prayers, or accumulate laws and activities to create it. All one needs to do is unveil it.

This chapter is about possibilities. To appreciate possibilities, it is essential that you not presume to understand anything about the truth, about Buddhism, about Zen, about God, about the hereafter, about reincarnation, about life. You must not presume that you can speak on any of these topics

*Very important

with anyone with any level of authority. You must be someone who has repeatedly failed in your life and is willing to continue failing for however long it takes to succeed. You must listen. You must be open to the anatomy of your own Buddha nature.

One of the hardest things for me to teach is the issue of paradigm and context living. In fact, in the thirty-some years that I have taught, I am continually impressed by the fact that most people have no idea about these issues. Everyone, without exception, has a personal paradigm of life; we also live within a universal context. Street people have to know about context living if they're going to survive. See, the first thing you want to do if you end up on the street tomorrow is to find the nearest street person. They'll tell you how to survive in the street, but you won't bother doing that because you've read a self-help book on the subject.

The context of our lives determines the circumstances, the situations, the people, the job and the quality of our lives. It is the paradigm of our lives. There is nothing in the universe that does not operate out of a paradigm. It's all about paradigms. In the search for freedom, we need to understand this.

There's a wonderful story that a friend of mine told me many years ago. It's a story about rats and people. An experiment was conducted in an effort to determine the differences between rats and people. The scientists conducting the experiment developed a maze in which they created three tunnels. They put a piece of cheese in the first tunnel. Then they put a rat into the maze to see what it would do. The rat immediately went down the first tunnel. He found the cheese, ate it and was satisfied. So they took the rat out of the maze and put cheese down the second tunnel. They put the rat back in. He ran down the first tunnel, saw there was no cheese, came out of that tunnel, ran down the second tunnel and found the cheese. They took the rat out of the maze again and put cheese down the third tunnel. The rat ran down the first tunnel because that's where he found the cheese the first time. He came back out and ran down the second tunnel because that's where he found the cheese the second time. It wasn't there. He came out and ran down the third tunnel, found the cheese and ate it.

The scientists repeated this experiment many times because they wanted to make sure that they weren't just dealing with a smart rat. Every single time, wherever they put the cheese, a given rat would eventually go down the correct tunnel. The difference between rats and humans is this: the rat will always go down the tunnel with the cheese; humans will go down the first tunnel and upon not finding the cheese the second time, will complain. The rat won't complain; he will just go down the next tunnel. He doesn't look up and say, "Hey! Where did you put the cheese?" The human will continue to complain because what the human will eventually do is believe in the tunnel because that is what humans do. Humans believe in tunnels. Even if there is no cheese, even if they are starving to death, they will keep going down the first tunnel. Even if the cheese is right next door in the second tunnel, they will stay in the first tunnel because that is where they found the cheese the first time. It was delicious; it was fun; and they know it's going to show up in that tunnel again some day!

We then take possession of the tunnel. We are waiting for the cheese to show up. What we don't understand is the nature of cheese. In effect, what we don't understand is freedom and what it takes to be truly free. That is what we don't understand, and this is what we are exploring here. Freedom. This is the paradigm for freedom of all Buddhas. What is a Buddha? A truly free being. If you bring your beliefs into the process of understanding context, and I don't care what the beliefs are, they will make it that much more difficult for you. If you persist in debating with me about the tunnel, it will take you that much longer to learn anything. Remember, I've got the cheese, and I know exactly where I'm going to put it. You have got to be interested only in finding the cheese. Then you can say that you are as smart as a rat. That's what we want. We want to be as smart as a rat because the rat will always get the cheese. Human beings care about the tunnel, about beliefs; they care about knowing. They care about being able to talk about what they think they "know." Rats care only about cheese. Rats care only about freedom. They know that cheese will provide them with the means for freedom.

The context within which most of us live our lives has to do with the paradigm of doing and having. This is a context that we learned early in our lives. When you were born, you were born as a Buddha. You need only to watch a child for about the first two years. You know why doctors call it the terrible twos? Because it is terrible for the child! That's when the adults start to mess them up, when they start to put the illusion of the tunnel in their minds. That's when adults start to talk to kids about the importance of having a tunnel. "You've got to have a tunnel! If you don't have a tunnel, you're not going to make it." That's what we start to tell our kids because that's what was told to us somewhere around our second year. Before that, we don't care about tunnels, we only care about the cheese and what we know is that the cheese can be found anywhere if we look hard enough. Some of you think that you have to go out and get a new tunnel. You look for tunnels, for books to read, for gurus to follow. These are all tunnels. The very notion that we can find freedom on your own leaves us at about the second year of our lives. Somewhere around then we begin to forget our own nature, we begin to forget who we are.

Jesus told his students to behold the birds of the air and the lilies of the field; they neither toil nor reap yet they always seem to have enough. They don't have savings accounts and 401K's and yet they have everything need. And we keep changing the environment on them! You go into New York City or Philadelphia and you find pigeons saying, "Okay, we have no trees, so we'll use your buildings." They find a way. When we begin to forget who we are, we also begin to believe in our limitations. We begin to believe in our limitations so much that if you listen to people's conversations, you will hear them talking exclusively about their limitations. I mean, just sit down and listen to people's conversations. What are they always talking about? Those issues in life that have got us bugged. Our limitations. A pigeon says, "Let's see; I've got a tin can; I've got some dirty tissue; I've got some string; I'll build my nest with these things and live on a ledge." But human beings say, "Yuck! We need a tunnel! We need a house. We need a ton of money."

And so, we enter the paradigm of Western civilization, if you want to call it that. The paradigm of forgetfulness -- the paradigm of fear is what it really is. And this is probably the most accurate description of the context of most people's lives. The paradigm of fear consists of the belief that in order to have, we must do something. You'll notice that most of our daily living consists in doing. You're doing all the time. I've got to go to work. I've got to do the wash. I've got to do this; I've got to do that. When someone calls you, they ask, "What are you doing?" Of course they ask you what you're doing because that's all you're ever doing is doing! Doing, doing, doing. Doing what? Why do you do all of that? Well, I've got to have money. I've got to have acceptance. I've got to have love. If I don't have this stuff, I'm in trouble.

So, our lives are about doing and we do it well. We do a lot of doing. We've been doing enough doing long enough to really know how to do it. We are experts at doing. Whatever it is you give me to do, I will do it. But I will not do it unless there is something to get from it. We don't just do anything in life. The unenlightened mind, in the paradigm of doing, having and being, does things only to have things. How many of you would go to that job you hate if you weren't getting paid, if it didn't provide you with your car insurance, with the money for your house, the vacation? How many of you are prepared to walk into your boss's office on Monday and say, "No more pay. I'll do this for free." They won't let you work. They'll say that you are

74

no longer an employee and that they don't use volunteers at their company. If the conversation goes on long enough they will call security and have you removed because you are crazy. Nobody does something for nothing!

Our doing is about having and we are convinced that if we do enough and have enough, we can then be. The paradigm of fear is doing and having in order to be. We are convinced that in order to be, we must do and have. This is the paradigm of fear that we learn or begin to develop in early childhood. It's a very powerful paradigm, so don't make light of it. It has you. It runs you.

Suggest to Zen students that they forget anything they have in their lives, and this includes people, and watch the swords appear. The swords are the excuses. If you listen to people's conversations, the way they defend themselves always is with what? What is our defense? In the old days, people pulled out their swords and shields. You do too. What are our weapons? Excuses. "See, the only reason why I really can't give my all to this practice is because I've got to do all this stuff. You don't understand Roshi, if I don't do this stuff, I can't have." Here is the excuse that I love the most: "And you know that if I don't have stuff, then I can't donate money to the monastery."

It is the context of one's life that determines what appears. The paradigm of fear is the compulsion to do and have in order to be. In that paradigm, I do almost everything I do, including meditation, to get something. I meditate to get what? To become enlightened; to be more peaceful; to be a better person. You see? In the paradigm of fear, I'm always doing something in order to have something. I am always doing something to have an event occur because I am convinced that if I work hard enough, if I do it long enough, I will eventually have it, and if I have it, then I can be. Look at the relationships between men and women in the family. This is the governing paradigm. I wonder how the human race got this far. Civilization has been around for only about five thousand years, but human beings have been on the planet for many thousands of years. We have come to believe that civilization is only about doing things and having things so that we can just be. I wonder how we engaged the act of being before that.

If you are attempting to discover whether or not your paradigm is one of fear, you need to only take a look at how much investment you have into doing and having. How much of your life is about collecting? The "workaholic" is nothing more than a person of fear. The "loveaholic" is nothing more than a person of fear. If you are giving all of your love to someone, do them a favor. Don't. I'm talking about those of you who are strangling the other person with love. Let them remember a time when they were just being themselves.

If you really want to love someone, give them the opportunity to remember a time when they didn't need you. That's scary, isn't it? What if they do remember! I suggest to you that even in the most profound and wonderful activities of life, such as loving another human being, we see the paradigm of fear when we really have the courage to look at and see it. How much of our loving others is about keeping them around? Maybe we are convinced that we cannot exist without them. That person who is trying to convince you how much you need them, is really trying to convince themselves how much they need you. They are really trying to support their conclusion that without you, they can't be.

In the paradigm of fear, everybody loses. In the paradigm of fear, conflict, dissatisfaction, pain and relationships that don't really work always appear. The person is always looking to do something new. When the doing doesn't work after a while, then we move into finding something better.

Dissolving the Paradigms

In the paradigm of a Buddha's life, doing and having things have nothing to do with being and yet a Buddha always has what is needed. One place to begin understanding this is with Shakespeare's words, "To thine own self be true." To this end, what is important is that you understand the paradigm of your life. What really manages you? How many of you can still not be totally committed to achieving your own awakening because you have all this stuff to do? How many of you still cannot let go because if you let go of what you have now, you are convinced that you will no longer exist. Some of my students say to me, "Well, if I forget my self, then what's left?" The paradigm of fear preoccupies us with egocentric perception. It's always about what is tangible for you. You've got this lifestyle that you can see. You have this and that. But what have you got? Anyone who comes along and even suggests the slightest possibility of giving any of that stuff up is the last person with whom we want to spend any real time.

The paradigm of fear would have us looking for happiness outside of ourselves. The paradigm of a Buddha's life is the Four Noble Truths. The context of a Buddha's life begins with the realization that life is suffering. Life is difficult. Life is birth and death. Life is change. You don't need me to tell you that. For those of you who keep looking for some kind of utopia, Buddhism says to you that there is no such place, so come out of the sky. The Buddha realized that there is a cause for our suffering. Few of us live in environments where we are lucky to get a bowl of rice in the course of our day, so we can't talk about the suffering that those followers of the Buddha experience. The kind of suffering that we can talk about is the mental conflict that is always going on: stress, worry, self doubt – all of the stuff that shows up in the context of fear.

The Buddha said in the Third Noble Truth that suffering can and should be eliminated. This is why one follows the Buddha way; why one chooses to follow the footsteps of the Buddha, why one chooses to be a Buddha in the world -- to find the causes for suffering and to eliminate them. The Fourth Noble Truth is the way to do this. It is referred to as the Eightfold Path. It begins with having the right context. No matter what you do, without right understanding, right view, right context, there is no possibility for liberation. None. The path to eliminating suffering in your life and in the lives of all the many beings in the world must start with having the right view of the world, the right view of yourself. You need to know that your paradigm redefines you at a young age. Another way of saying this is that what appears to be your life is not your life. What life appears to be for most of us is not our lives. Most of us live with the perception of life, not with life itself. We don't live with life as it is.

We need to recognize that the beginning of liberation and the elimination of the cause of suffering in the Eightfold Noble Path of the Buddha is having the right understanding, the right context. One of the problems for us is that we automatically presume that simply because we go to school that we are learning something. We are beginning to see that we must give up that presumption more and more each day. Unfortunately, we are learning it the hard way. We're waiting for the product to come out of the school. We are finally beginning to say that just because the student is in the classroom doesn't imply that they have learned anything, especially Zen students. One of the presumptions of Buddhist students is that just because they are in the zendo, they are learning something. People say, "Life is a learning experience." Usually people who say that have not learned very much in life. When you've really learned that life is suffering, there's very little you can say about it, including walking up to someone who's suffering and saying, "Don't worry, life is a learning experience." It's like going to the funeral of a woman who has just lost her husband after sixty years of a passionate, loving relationship and saying, "Don't worry, everything will be alright." You do that with me and I'll kick your ass out of the temple.

The path to liberation, the path to freedom, begins with right understanding, with right context. When we talk about the Six Perfections or the Six Paramitas, we can say that we are talking about the six qualities that form the context of a Buddha's life. We just described certain aspects of that context. Life is suffering. Suffering has a source; it has a cause. The causes of suffering can be and should be eliminated. The way to eliminate the causes of suffering begins with and ends with the right context. The right context is that all beings are Buddha. "All beings" comprise everything. Another way of saying this is that the universe and everything in it is Buddha. What do we mean? That the universe and everything in it lacks nothing. The universe and everything in it does not need you or me to add anything to it or take anything away from it. The universe was working fine until we came along and thought about it.

So the context within which we can begin to understand what these Paramitas are about begins with your seeing your perfection. It's very dangerous to use the word "perfection." My students have heard me say this over and over again – "Do not believe a word of what I say." My use of certain terms is not what you think it is, especially the use of the word "perfect." In Buddhism the word "perfect" is meant to mean "just as it is." In order to understand the phrase "just as it is", we need to look at what "it" means. "It" has to do with the nature of life, the nature of everything in the universe. When I, a student of the Dharma, look at the universe, what do I see? A rat can answer that question instantly. Rats look for what is there. It takes us a little longer to do this because what we immediately refer to is our "knowledge," all of the stuff that we have collected over the years, what we think we know. When I ask you what you see, you refer to your perceptions, your beliefs, your ideas, and your conclusions about the world. That is why the masters have said no eye can see this and no ear can hear it. The eyes and the ears that they are referring to is the ego mind, the discriminating mind that is always looking at things and comparing them to some idea.

Ego mind or small mind as it is often referred to in Buddhism, is always in the mode of judgment, assessment and comparison. That is its nature. It is always comparing what it is viewing to something else and measuring it relative to that. When we look at the universe with the ego mind, we can't see this activity. If you read this with your discriminating mind, if you are saying to yourself, "Well, I don't know about that; I don't think I like that," then you will not understand any of this. Right understanding transcends all the information in your data banks. It's not in them. It's not in the source of your suffering. It's not in what is causing the suffering in your life, but small mind is the instrument that we use to try to understand this. It's like putting a fox in a hen house to protect the hens from other foxes. We use our intellect in order to solve problems of the spirit and that never works. That's putting the cart before the horse. We need to develop the means to understand this misuse of small mind. For example, notice what happens within you when I say, "The nature of the universe is that nothing lasts. Nothing is permanent."

Everything is impermanent. Everything is constantly changing. That being the case, ask yourself, "What are you holding into? Why are you so afraid of letting go? What is it that you really think you have and why do you spend your days holding on to it?" Open your hand and you will find that it is empty. There's nothing there.

An abbot and a novice lived in a Benedictine Monastery that depended a great deal on its benefactors. In fact, when you went in the front door you faced a huge room on whose walls were the names of all the benefactors. One day, shortly after one of the major benefactors had died, the novice was put in charge of keeping the room clean and the plaques polished. He walked into the room to find out where he was to put the name of this particular benefactor, and in the course of his conversation with the Abbot, he asked the Abbot, "What did he leave, Father?" the Abbot looked at him and said, "Everything, of course." The ego mind cannot grasp this. What did the benefactor take with him? Nothing. Do you notice how we hold onto stuff as if it belongs to us and that we will have it forever? Everything is changing, so what are you trying to hold onto? What are you trying to keep the same? The nature of everything in the universe is impermanence. You are changing. I am changing. When someone asks you who you are, what can you truthfully say? Nothing. The moment you conclude who you are, you are caught in the big illusion. So what are you trying to protect about yourself right now? Whatever it is, it's going to change.

One of the causes for suffering is spiritual constipation. Most of us are constipated. There are a lot of constipated people on spiritual paths. One day, all of those people are going to wake up and they will make the loudest fart you'll ever hear. What happens when we are constipated? Something is blocking the path. In this respect, we are our worst enemies. We get in the way of what is true about us. What we always bring to our relationships is this idea of who we are. When you think about this, you must ask the question, "With whom are we in relationship?" I did not begin to really understand the nature of love until I was willing to give up my ideas about love. You can't begin to understand love until you give up your expectations. Freedom requires the letting go of your expectations of whatever shows up in your life. Love is nothing more than the manifestation of a truly free person. Only a free person can love another being. Someone who is not attached to what they want, to what they feel, to what they think can truly love another human being. This is difficult to do.

Until we liberate ourselves from our preconceptions, the best we can do is to be authentic about our inauthenticity. We love others to be loved, and that's not what loving is. Did you ever notice how all of the great lovers in literature, Don Juan and all of them, were always risking their lives? All of the great lovers were risking their lives to love someone else. Why did the authors write about risk? Why does the "Greatest Story Ever Told" include, in the end, the death of the great lover Jesus Christ? Why did the Buddha have to leave comfort and security and great wealth and possessions in order to realize nirvana?

When we talk about Buddha nature, we understand that it always expresses itself as a set of virtues or if you don't like the word virtue then as universal laws, natural truths. This is to say that wherever I look, I can see Buddha nature expressing itself as a virtue, as a universal truth. I can see it everywhere. You can see it. When we talk about the perfections of a Buddha, when we talk about the qualities of Buddha nature, we are talking about these particular virtues or truths. The way we do it in the paradigm of fear is that we will take these virtues and do them. We are not talking about doing anything here. When a Buddha is present, these perfections manifest themselves naturally. The nature of freedom is innate generosity, virtuous effort, renunciation, wise effort, transcendent wisdom, patience, truthfulness, devotion, loving kindness and equanimity. These are the qualities of Buddha nature. Buddha nature is always expressing itself in these qualities or Paramitas. This is your true nature. This is how you start out.

As I just mentioned, these virtues are not something you can do. If you try to do them, you will find that you always come short. This is not about doing. These are not the ten steps to becoming a Buddha. If you are reading this carefully, you will know that deep inside you are a Buddha. It is there. It's underneath the trappings of your life. You must learn how to dig in a way that you find that vein of gold. Buddhism says that all beings possess these qualities innately, that this is the whole universe.

If this is who you are, if this is the gold beneath the shanty, what we are saying is that these virtues arise from the spiritual development or refinement of one's practice. It's like knowing that ten feet below you is a vein of gold; we now have to get to it. The cultivation of the Paramitas is a means of unveiling or uncovering your Buddha nature. So they are both your Buddha nature and the means of uncovering your Buddha nature. To practice the Paramitas is something like faking it until you get it. In the practicing of them, you are

81

shoveling the dirt away to get to that vein of gold. Within every being, we find these perfections. Now remember, this word "perfection" does not mean utopia. How does perfection express it self in the universe?

Perfection expresses itself as change. So if you want to be perfect, then change. The truth of the matter is that you will change regardless of what you are clinging to. You'll change one way or another. Some of you will just go through life constipated and then change when you die, but you'll change. In Buddhism death is the great liberator. It's the one that stands before you after all those years of your pointless striving.

Your Buddha nature is the undisturbed part of your being. Throughout our lives we have those moments where we have the experience of absolute contentment. We are content to just be. Maybe it's when we are walking in the mountains, maybe it's when we are observing a beloved one and we're content simply to look at them. We don't need to get them to do anything for us. We don't need them to act any way. In those moments you have glimpsed the gold. In Zen we call this kensho, or the first awakening. You have looked into your nature. You have seen it. And then you do what you always do. You think about it and the moment you think about it, it is gone. It's like Tinkerbelle following Peter Pan everywhere. The moment certain things happened, she was gone. Buddha nature is the same way. It is within you at all times. It is your true nature and what you have done over the years is to cover it with the trappings, with the illusions, with the fear that blinds us. Buddha nature is not learned. Your parents don't teach it to you and neither does society, the church, Buddha or God. All of the reading in the world doesn't give it to you; it is already there.

The first of the Paramitas is innate generosity or Dana. Most of us perceive generosity as my giving you something to you that you don't have. I'm the elevated one in that relationship. I'm the one who has something and I bestow it to you. That's how most of us think about generosity. I am a generous person, so I go and I give to those who don't have anything. Remember that your definitions of the terms we use to identify Buddha nature don't work. So what I'm saying is that this is not innate generosity. The practice of Dana has nothing to do with your giving your abundance to those who have little because there is no one who has little and no one who has more. All beings possess Buddha nature, lacking nothing. They don't need you to add anything to them. They don't need your help unless it is the right kind of help, they do need your help if you have the right kind of help

Loving someone is about being in a relationship in which you help another person to reach his or her fullest potential. In a really powerful relationship, the parties involved give up making the other person wrong and, as I just mentioned, of doing everything necessary for the beloved one to reach his or her fullest potential. Sometimes that expresses itself in this way: "What do you want to do? What do you really want to do?"

"Well, I really want to be an artist, but I've got all these bills and I've got to go to work…"

"No, no no. You go and pursue your art. I'll take care of the bills. I'll work so that you can realize your fullest potential as a great artist if that is what you really need to do to be a whole person. I've been watching you. You go to work and you are miserable then you come home at night and we fight."

Perhaps there will be times when I resent making this agreement with you, but I vow to be big enough to be able to hold my resentment as my part of the bargain. If you aren't big enough to make the sacrifice, shut up and get out of the way. Don't offer it.

In the Book of Ephesians in the New Testament, there's a passage about making promises you can't keep. It goes something like this: God views someone who makes a promise they can't keep as a fool. Jesus says to say yes when you mean yes and no when you mean no. Everything else is a lie. You are going to have to risk your paradigm of what it means to be generous. You have to be willing to look beyond the idea that, "I will share my abundance with you." That's not what the Buddha's paradigm of generosity is about. It's more like this: everything is changing; therefore, whatever I have is not mine anyway. It will be gone. Break out the booze and have a ball. You need me to forgive you? I forgive you because my feelings are not mine anyway. That might surprise some of you. Think about it. Who wants to be in a relationship with someone who is always feeling animosity? One thing I know about my feelings is that they will change. Truly wise people do not attach themselves to complaint or praise. I know you will always find something wrong with me and, in between, you will find something right about me. From the perspective of Buddhism, generosity operates out of the understanding that everything is changing, everything is impermanent; therefore what I have is not mine and I'm going to have to let go of it one day. Why not let go of it now while I really can use it to create a powerful relationship because those I value may not be here tomorrow.

When Mother Theresa was training her postulants to go into Calcutta and do the work of her order, she would say to them, "Let them eat you up."

Let them consume you. Give them everything they need and want. Let them take it all until you have nothing left. Then you will understand my joy. Then you will understand why I have been doing this work most of my life. The Paramita of generosity has us ask the question, "What really brings you joy." How many of us can relate to this story? When I was a kid, about sixteen years old, I had my driver's license and I was really convinced that a brand new GTO was really what I needed to be happy. My father is a very wise man, so he gave me one that was about ten years old. He actually did not give it to me; he found it for me and I bought it. When I sat in that car, I knew that life was wonderful. I was The Man. This girl came along and she wanted to go to dinner and she wanted to do this and she wanted to do that, and I really wanted to be with her. But I was putting sixty to eighty bucks' worth of gas into this car every week. I only got paid one hundred bucks a week. And then something strange happened. The car began to be a problem. How many of us know that that is true? How many shirts can you wear at one time? How many pieces of jewelry? How big a house do you really need?

So I ask you, what really brings you joy? I want you to look at the times in your life when you really were joyful, when you were really happy. I don't know about you, but for me it was when I finally sold the GTO and used the money to make my girlfriend happy. When you really have the courage to let go of what you're holding onto, you will know that what really makes us joyful and contented is loving someone else -- not in the way that we're accustomed to doing it, but in the way that the Paramita of generosity would have us do it. What brings us joy is living in harmony with our innate generosity. A baby throws itself at us, doesn't it? It gives us everything it's got, even some stuff we don't want. It's trying to help you remember who you really are.

Some of you are still wrestling with your practice because you have really not given your whole being to it. You're still holding on to something. You think that the Roshi just doesn't understand you because he lives isolated at that monastery. He doesn't have to deal with people, he doesn't have parents, he doesn't have the flu... Do you ever notice how when it's us, it's as if no one else has ever been through these things before? No one else has ever had to deal with them. The ego mind has you convinced that you cannot practice. The ego mind is the context for your life and it limits you to seeing the reality of things. It has us convinced in those moments that we are the only ones who have ever faced these problems. The truth of the matter is that when we are living in harmony with our true nature, with these Paramitas, something begins to happen to us. Something begins to happen to our relationships.

Something begins to happen to our environment. Generosity engenders a natural compassion for all beings. What is compassion for all beings? It is the ability to look into any being and see its fullest potential for freedom and Buddhahood. Generosity always expresses itself as steadfastness. My container is big enough to deal with the fact that while you're hiking in the Himalayas I've still got that college debt of yours to pay off and I would really like to do some vacationing myself! But generosity is not really like that. It's more like saying, "That's what I said I would do for you." We'll talk more about that when we discuss the heart of renunciation.

Generosity always expresses itself as devotion. The lover is truly devoted to the beloved. Everybody can see it. They really love each other. Generosity is not about doing things. It is about tapping into the vein of gold, about tapping into your innate quality. You need to know that these are descriptions of energy. The energy called generosity prevents us from saying, "I just don't know how much more I can take of this." If you embody the Paramita of generosity, then you will deal with it, you can deal with it. "I don't know if I'll survive." That's whining. You will cope with things and even if you don't, what are you trying to protect? So you don't survive. Guess what? You die. Now you don't have to worry about anything. What are you really afraid to let go of?

Generosity is not about doing. It is a universal law. When we look at nature, especially in the changing of the seasons, we see innate generosity. Nature is always giving things up. Everything else in the universe lets go except human beings. Everything. Everything around us is not only willing, but is actively participating in the Paramita of generosity. When you tap into the innate generosity of your Buddha nature, you will always have what you need… and more. In the paradigm of fear, you think you have to find a better job that will give you more money, even if you don't like the job, until you get what you want. When you tap into innate generosity and you will be able to say yes to everything.

When I, a student of Dharma, look at the real form of the universe I see this innate generosity. You need my arm, take my arm. You need my time, take my time. Generosity is an expression of real freedom. One of the powerful stories in my life has to do with Jesus. I think about the evening of his arrest. The Romans went to Gethsemane, they dragged him to jail and they took his clothes from him. He put up no resistance.

"People say you are the Christ. Are you the Christ?"

"Well, if you say so."

"I have the power to set you free."

"No you don't."

"I'm going to kill you."

"Maybe. We'll see."

I don't mean that Jesus was cocky as if he knew what was going to happen to him. He didn't know. There was a good chance that everything they said about him wasn't true. Nonetheless they dragged him through the streets and humiliated him. He lost his friends. He offered no defense.

In Zen, there's a wonderful story about an old man who lived at the edge of a village and how one day his heart goes out compassionately to a young girl he found on the streets. He takes her into his home. He lets her live with him. He didn't know that the girl was promiscuous and one day the girl goes out and gets pregnant. The word goes out throughout the village that the old man impregnated her. It's the old man's baby. The townspeople come to the old man's house one night with torches. The girl is afraid for her reputation and what might happen to her. When the townspeople accuse the man, he says nothing. Now you have to remember that the old man begins with compassion for the girl. He knows that if he denies the accusations then the girl will be in trouble. He says nothing, so they take all of his belongings and burn his house down. The following morning he is seen in the rubble of his old house with a cooking pot that survived the fire. He uses the remaining fire to cook his morning soup and tea. Several days later he's still there. This time the girl comes back with the townspeople. Their tails are between their legs, their heads are lowered and they say that the young girl told them the truth. It wasn't he who impregnated her. They apologize and the man silently continues to drink his tea. The crowd starts to walk away and the girl follows them. The old man says to the girl, "Where are you going?" She tells him that she's not sure. She has nowhere to go. And he says, "Yes you do. Would you like some tea?" This is freedom. Take my house. Take my dignity.

I often refer to the scene from the movie "Braveheart" where Mel Gibson rides in front of his retreating armies and says, "They may take our lives, but they will never take our freedom." We have a really perverted understanding of freedom. We think it is something that is given to us. Freedom is not given to us. No one can give it to us and no one can take it from us if we are truly free. If we are truly free, they can burn down our house and take everything, including our lives, and it doesn't mean anything. How do you arrive at that type of freedom? How do you truly become free in life so that no matter what shows up you are big enough to hold it? You see, if the context of your life is just about you then you are not big enough to handle true freedom. It doesn't take a genius to know this. Just listen to people's conversations. Just ask somebody to do something that is going to require some effort and you'll know where they're coming from.

Unlimited Generosity

In the ego-centric perception of the universe, the spiritual container is very small. You know how fear feels when it's got you. Franklin D. Roosevelt said, "We have nothing to fear, but fear itself." What he actually meant was that we have nothing to fear but our perception of fear. We really think that what we see is what is going on, but it's not. With the right perspective, you can be in the most devastating, frightening situations and still be able to handle them. When life gets difficult, what do most of us do? We want to retreat. We want to step back and send up the flag of limitations. How does the ego mind respond to any given circumstance when it shows up? This small mind that exists in the paradigm of fear always responds in the same way to no matter what shows up. The first thing the ego mind does is review its limitations.

The ego mind really perceives itself as a bundle of limitations. I want you to see this. I want you to see how the ego mind operates within the paradigm of fear. It's not as if you are a bad person. If you don't know how the paradigm of fear operates and if you are trapped in it, then all that you perceive is your limitations.

When I first started conducting life-seminar programs some twenty years ago, a girl brought her mother to one of them. As part of the program, I conducted a healing exercise for pain relief. During a break, she asked if I would use her mother as a subject. She said that her mother suffered from terrible migraine headaches and that their family had had a terrible time with them over the years. The mother agreed to do it. I sat her in front of me and we went through a kind of meditation. I asked the audience to look at their pain, describe it, and so forth. When we got to the point where we induce pain relief, the mother jumped out of her chair and started yelling at me. She said, "You can't have my headache. It's all I've got!" After that weekend, she never suffered from migraine headaches again simply because she realized what the pain really meant to her, her daughter and their family. You see, most of us worship our limitations. Our limitations are our gods. They run our lives. They are also our saviors. Whenever we don't want to face something we can say, "Look at my limitations!" One of the reasons why people don't spend too much time with Roshis is that they'll say to you that they don't care about limitations.

We need to look at how we operate at all times. We must begin with a willingness to tell the truth. You must start acknowledging that you live for your limitations. This is probably your paradigm. My life is about my limitations. What limitations do you bring to the relationships of your life? You need to know that your limitations are never who you truly are. You have, however, chiseled them in stone. Are they not therefore real? They're very real …for you. But consider this. Roshis have mothers. Roshis have bills. Roshis have personal relationships. Roshis have headaches. They have all of that. Outwardly, nothing changes for them. They just hold these things differently than do most people.

Freedom is not about having the circumstances of your life change so you can be free. Freedom is expressed in an unlimited way of living. Do you know the New Testament parable about the fish and the loaves of bread? What is that story about? Do you really think that it was literal? You need to look at the whole story. There's much more to it. It's about relationships. It's about innate generosity. Two people who truly love each other can give one another pieces of paper with something they drew on it for their anniversary and they will cherish them. Then you came along and say, "That's all he gave you for your anniversary? That cheapskate! How much money does he make?" But to the beloved it's everything. Life is never what it appears to be.

Generosity is an expression of freedom. In order to practice innate generosity, in order to tap into that vein of gold, you have to begin to let go. You have to let go. You have to. Otherwise your limitations will stay with you and you will be buried with them. After your death, people won't talk about you; they'll talk about your limitations. "Every time I called him he always had an excuse." That's what they'll remember. They won't remember you, they'll remember your excuses. In today's world, a person's word is equal to their excuses. In order to realize your unlimited potential, in order to realize real freedom for yourself, you have to begin to start letting go of whatever it is you are holding onto.

I don't think we appreciate the energy of innate generosity. Take a moment to recall a time in your life when someone came to you and gave you something that you experienced to be exceptionally generous. Keep that memory with you. Try to recall with it how you felt. Now I want you to remember a time in which someone withheld something from you. Maybe you were a kid. You went to your parents for help and they told you they didn't have enough time for you. Notice the energy in that experience. Now I want you to remember a time when you were extremely generous. Maybe you were in love and you were willing to do anything for your beloved. You were willing to give up your expectations. Even when he or she really screwed up, you were willing to forgive it. Remember how that felt. Now I want you to remember a time when you were unwilling to forgive. You wanted to make sure that the persons paid what they owed you for screwing up so badly. Recall how that felt.

Everything in life: every thought, every word, every action is energy manifesting itself as thought, as word, as deed. Everything is energy. If we put you under a microscope, we see the dance of matter and energy. That's what you are. You think you are that person there with that name and that body and those thoughts when you are really a pocket of energy manifesting itself as that form. Every thought is a form of energy that produces a particular result. So when you recalled being generous or someone's being generous with you, you got a sense of what innate generosity can generate in your life. Think of yourselves as electrical sockets. Most of us say: "I've got electricity." But all we are is a bare socket with nothing plugged into it. "But I've got electricity." Okay. Are you ever going to use it? No! Why should I? If I use it, then I may not have any more electricity. But if you don't plug anything into the socket, what does it matter if you've got electricity? I can say that all beings are Buddhas and most of you will agree with me. But if people don't practice their Buddha nature it doesn't mean anything anymore than the fact that I have electricity and don't use it. Now, I also want you to know that innate generosity is just like electricity. If I go over to a socket and stick my finger in it, it will knock me on my ass. If I get up and stick my finger in it again, it will knock me on my ass again. Innate generosity and the practice of it are like electricity. Every time you tap into it, the same results occur. So, if you wonder whether or not you are practicing innate generosity, remember that it is just like electricity -- you will know. The people and the environment will be transformed.

When the student and the teacher come together for dokusan, a private meeting, and the teacher asks the student, "What is the essence of Buddhism?" and the student says, "The essence of Buddhism is blah blah blah blah blah..." the teacher rings the bell and the student must leave because he is missing the point of practice and of Buddhism. Students are always telling the roshi what they've read, what they've heard, and what they think. In our monastery, when you come to the dokusan room, you knock on the door. You've already answered me. I already know what you are going to bring me when you come in. It doesn't matter to me that you've got electricity. Have you plugged into it? Are you letting go? Are you sacrificing? You come to me and you say, "I've tried everything to get them to love me." I will tell you that you have not because what is natural to us is that we respond to innate generosity. We recognize it when it's present. It's like Mother Theresa's walking into Russia and opening up an AIDS clinic. She had no money to do this. But then people came along and suddenly there was enough money. People respond to the Mother Theresas of the world because Buddhas respond to Buddhas and Buddhas know Buddhas. So when you have truly tapped into the socket, it will knock you on your ass and you will know that you have touched electricity. When you truly tap into your innate generosity, you will always get the same results and you will always know it.

If you want to practice innate generosity, then this is how you do it. If someone comes along and asks you for something, give it to them. If someone needs to be forgiven, forgive them. How many times? As Jesus said, "Seventy times seventy times seventy." Jesus was a Roshi too. He knew that he had to give some kind of answer. But he also knew that it didn't matter what he said because the person asking the question would not understand it anyway. Do you think that that person went off and started forgiving everyone? No. If you have to ask the question, you won't get the answer. So, how do you realize the answer to the question? Give, give, give. "But I don't have anything left," you reply. Give more. "But I've given everything," you insist. No you haven't. If we start examining our capacity for generosity, we will find there is always more to give. What do I have to give? Maybe my life.

There is a wonderful story of the Buddha during one of his incarnations. He was the Bodhisattva Avalokitesvara – the enlightened being of compassion. He was wandering in the forest one day and over a cliff he heard lion cubs crying. He looked over and he saw the mother. There had been a great drought in the area for a long time and there was no food to gather. The babies were emaciated and the mother was doing her best to feed them. They were going to die if they didn't get any food. He thought, "What can I do?" He looked around and there was nothing left. All the food was gone. Finally, he made his way down the cliff. The lions were too weak to do anything so they allowed him to sit with them. The story goes that Avalokitesvara, the Buddha incarnate, offered his own flesh to feed the lions because he realized he still had something to give -- himself.

The ego mind can't comprehend this. In the paradigm of fear, this makes no sense, none whatsoever. You can take that story seriously and perhaps one day one of you will be called to do just that, but the story is also a metaphor. Many of you withhold yourself from your relationships, don't you? Maybe all that will be needed is for you to be present. Maybe all that someone wants is for you to be around. It's like when the student says, "Well, I don't really have anything to ask in dokusan. Should I still go?" He or she just doesn't get it. It's not about what you will get when you come to dokusan. It's about what you bring to it. Give, give, give. But how do I know if I have anything to give? Well, the story just told you. How will you know if there's really nothing left to give?

You will be dead. George Bernard Shaw said, "My entire life belongs to the whole community and I wish to give to it whatever I can before I die. I want to be thoroughly used up before I die." Mother Theresa says, "Let them eat you up." Let them consume the very last drop of you and you will be free. Herod comes to John the Baptist. John says, "You must have come to set me free." Herod says, "No I have come to cut your head off." John says, "Then you have come to set me free." That's what Mother Theresa and George Bernard Shaw and Avalokitesvara were pointing to.

What's true about us, what makes us perfect, is the fact that we are both infinite, unlimited beings and limited at the same time. It's not enough to just practice generosity, we must practice wisely. We must never engage in fear-based generosity. What is true about me is that I am both limited and unlimited at the same time. That's what perfection is. Perfection isn't just one sided. You can't talk about the unlimited without talking about the limited. The only way that I am able to do what I am able to do is to tell you that I am a limited being with unlimited capabilities. Figure that one out. You can't. But I will tell you that what is true about you and me is that we are limited, finite beings who are infinite and eternal. Sometimes giving means receiving. Sometimes our innate generosity must express itself in our willingness to receive from others. How many of you never receive anything from anybody? You're cool, you can handle it, you don't need anybody's help; you practice Zen. You are a Zen warrior. You don't need to be loved. Roshis don't need to be loved. My students think that they don't need to respect me because I'm a Roshi, that I can handle it. They think, "I don't need to appreciate him; I can leave. He's unlimited and floats around the monastery." Sometimes the most generous thing that we can offer to other people is our brokenness. Let them have the glory of helping others for a change. They'll remember you for it.

How does generosity translate in our relationships with our children? We have to stop trying to live their lives. Get off the stage! The director has called them onto it, not you! But what if they forget their lines? They'll work harder to remember them the next time. If you let them work harder, they'll find out that they can do anything they want. Maybe the most generous thing we can do for our children is to just be there for them. Let them screw up royally. Just keep being there to encourage them in the knowledge that, even if they screw up all the time, they are still Buddhas. How much of our wanting to do things for them is really wanting to do things for ourselves? We don't want the reputation of having a bad kid. God forbid if the village finds out we've got a bad kid.

Sometimes our innate generosity can manifest in the world by our just getting out of the way. For some of you, the most generous thing that you can give to life is to die. The most important thing for you to do in your life will be to die because then you'll be out of the way. This is how generosity sometimes expresses itself. In the Buddha way, I am no one; you don't need me. If you want my help, it is there, but you have to call for it. The Zen master simply says, "This is what you've got to do. If you don't want to do it, good-bye." I've never chased a student who has left and I never intend to. Some of us need to ask, "What do I have to share with others?" Maybe sometimes the sharing is just your presence, but you have something to share. There's no one who has nothing to share because if that were true, you wouldn't be reading this. The universe creates its forms, its manifestations for a purpose. There is a time and a purpose for everything under the sun. That includes you. Instead of managing your life so that you are trying to get pleasure and comfort all the time, you will find that when you begin to give, you will begin to get pleasure and comfort that you can't even imagine.

Generosity is not "me" giving to someone else. It is the recognition of our sameness. Jesus said, "Love your neighbor as yourself." What was he saying? That he is you. That she is you. We're all the same. From the

Roshi down to the postulant, we're all the same. We all feel pain; we've all got concerns to deal with; we all die. In my giving to you I am giving to myself. The only thing that makes relationships work is when both parties are focused on what the other needs. So if I'm taking care of your needs and you're taking care of my needs, then no one needs anything and we just dance together. We are all broken but perfect. Every one of us is broken, shattered, and perfect. The shatteredness and the brokenness of our lives is the essence of our perfection. I never learned a thing from having fun. I never learned a thing from being right. All my learning came from failure and mistakes, from pain and disappointment.

In order to have right view and right understanding, you need to transform your view of those things in your life that you resist the most. To tap into innate generosity, you must do the very thing you have resisted doing your whole life. Whatever it is that you keep telling people you can't do, go do it. No matter the price. No matter the cost. You want to be free? You say to me, "Roshi, make me free. I want to be me." I can't help you if you don't want to be you! In order to be you, there's a price to pay because you've got to give up your costume; you've got to get off the stage! That is scary business.

Innate generosity is the recognition that the universe lacks nothing, that it needs nothing. Whatever we need is already there. Everything is changing anyway, so why hold onto it? Give, give, give.

But there is something you need to understand about giving. You must give wisely. Another aspect of giving, which we seldom recognize, is being generous to yourself. Mother Theresa was no good to anyone unless she was present. The woman knew her limitations. That is why she enlisted postulants and novices and officers and a board and delegated power. It's not as if you empty your bank account and throw money out the window. A friend of mine used to say that this is how you save a sinking ship: one hand for yourself and one hand for the ship. If you get tossed overboard, the whole ship goes down. You see? The person who gives their all and never rests and never meditates and never eats right and never exercises is a fool.

You must know your limitations, but don't attach yourself to them. Say "yes" when you mean "yes" and "no" when you mean "no." Don't tell me you're going to do something that you are not going to do. The spirit cares only about flying; as to who does the flying it has but a passing interest. This is the nature of the universe. It is benignly indifferent. The world around us and in us could care less about your list of limitations. Only people who do not know who they are care about your list.

Do you ever listen to people in a restaurant? It's always limitation this, limitation that, got to have this, got to have that, need this, need that. And you wonder why we're so exhausted when we get home from work. I need a drink! I can't go to the monastery tonight! Of course you can't! Meditation does not work for you after a day of raping and stealing! And that's how most of us practice our Zen. I'm meditating, don't bother me! I've got to go and meditate! I told you to leave me alone!

The Heart Within

Having a virtuous heart implies that all Buddhas have a code of living. They are ethical beings. There is no possibility of being a Buddha apart from having a code of life. Why? When I look at the universe, everything is a function of a code. Everything operates according to paradigms. Everything is karma. Everything is relative. When you sit next to your beloved, two hours seems like two minutes. When you sit on a hot stove, two minutes seems like two hours. Everything follows a code of existence, of living. Even if the sun were to rise in the west, the Bodhisattva follows only one code. All Buddhas freely chose to act only within that code of life. They choose freely. What does that mean? If they screw up, they don't go crazy about it. They notice it and go back to their code of life. They don't sit around and say, "You know, I screwed up because my mother came over. You don't understand, I was just so tired that I couldn't get up for the sitting." It doesn't work that way. A Buddha states the truth. "I didn't want to go. The truth of the matter is that I'm a selfish little clod of ailments and grievances complaining that you don't make me happy enough. That's why I didn't come."

A code of living has to do with honor, loyalty, and that four-letter word – commitment -- the word that everybody fears. I want enlightenment, but don't ask me to commit. The Buddha is a committed being, a devoted being. From the domain of innate generosity, devotion and commitment means losing everything to achieve awareness and liberate others from suffering. The virtuous heart is loyal; it is devoted. Integrity is what Webster defines as "strict adherence to a particular way of being." When we talk about the virtuous heart, we talk about the practice of integrity. All of spiritual life rests upon the virtuous heart. There is no spiritual path without virtue, without integrity. You cannot believe in God without integrity. You cannot follow Christ without integrity. You cannot practice Buddhism without integrity. You cannot achieve any real awareness without integrity. You can't have a successful relationship without integrity. You can't do it, so forget it. All spiritual life rests on a virtuous life. The Buddha calls it the joy of integrity.

Gandhi changed the entire world, conquered an entire empire on one single devoted, committed truth: No matter what the British do, I will not respond with violence. When he was asked to define his revolution that is what he always said. No matter what happens to me I will not harm another human being. They imprisoned him, beat him and tortured him and he never raised a hand or spoke a word of malice. When his body was in pain and tortured and uncomfortable do you think it was difficult for him to practice that way? When Jesus viewed his mother and his friends and everyone else who was there from the cross do you think it was difficult for him to say, "Forgive them?" Do you think it was difficult for the Japanese who lost their grandparents at Hiroshima to forgive America? Do you think it's difficult when you're feeling rage in your relationships, when you are feeling really violated, to forgive? You're right, it is. But that's what makes a virtuous life as great as what it is. We want our greatness for nothing. We cannot have it for nothing and that is what makes it great. Every hero that we have ever worshipped either sacrificed his or her own life or sacrificed something else, but there is always a sacrifice. Why do we think we can be great without it? Why? Who do we think we are?

The person who does not practice with integrity does not convince me that they are serious about God, Buddha, Nirvana or anything. We need to be authentic about our own inauthenticity. We need to understand that integrity is difficult, especially in today's society. It's not easy at all to be virtuous, and yet it is who we are. The practice of living in harmony with our nature will set us free and will free others from suffering. We must come face to face with our practice and ask the question, "Am I truly devoted?" Devotion always manifests itself with a code of living. It is the ignorant Zen student who thinks that Zen -- and this is a very Western thing, you don't find this in Japan -- is the practice of "anything goes." Everything is Zen. It's all Buddha nature. But it doesn't mean that at all. The Buddha Shakyamuni and all Buddhas, Jesus, Gandhi, Mother Theresa, every single one of them had a code of living. They functioned in the paradigm of virtue.

There are three levels in the practice of the Paramita of virtue or the Paramita of a virtuous heart. The first is non-harming. This, believe it or not, is what Buddhism refers to as the human realm. I bet you think that you are human. Buddhism says, "Not necessarily." What makes us human is the choice to not harm another human being. That's what separates us from the animals. Until we arrive at the virtue of non-harming, we're not really human. In the practice of non-harming, it is the choice to refrain from activities that harm other beings. The Buddhist practices this in the domain of the precepts. What most Buddhist students don't understand when they receive the precepts is that the precepts, like the Paramitas, like the Eightfold Noble Path is Mahayanna -- the great vehicle. It is training. The practice of innate generosity, of the virtuous heart and the remaining Paramitas is your training. This is your refining. This is how you develop your Buddha nature. That training begins with the first precept not to kill other beings. When we say not to kill we mean not to kill by word, not to kill by thought, and not to kill by action. This is a very difficult precept. What about food? What about people in other nations who need food? What about "overpopulation" of the animal world? The New York Times once ran a comic strip in which two deer were in the forest standing next to a sign that said "Hunting Season Open." They were watching some hunters come up the road. The one deer said to the other, "Why the hell don't they thin out their own damn herd?" Is the problem really too many deer? You hear about that on the news these days. My father is a hunter. He says to me, "You know there are too many deer." He's always got to explain to me why he's goes hunting. There are too many deer. They're going take over the universe. They're going to march on Washington one of these days.

There's a wonderful story about Katagiri Roshi's Zen center. It was once overrun by roaches. Now, it's one thing to be sitting quietly as usual. It's quite another thing to be sitting and having a bug climb onto you. You really get to examine how you feel about that bug. But it had gotten to a point where the Roshi's officers came to him and asked, "Roshi, what do we do?" Katagiri Roshi turned to them and told them that he wasn't going to tell them. This is not about an absolute way of acting. This is not about an edict from God: Thou shall not kill. That's not what it's about. In Buddhism, you have to be willing to wrestle with your questions. You think the answer is the prize. It isn't. It's the activity of wrestling with the question, "What should I do?" The fool thinks, "Well, now I'll become a vegetarian." But you're still killing. What do you think you've done? What do you think the plant feels like? Is it right to kill corn? So what is this really about? What is really going on here? You won't know until you've wrestled with the question.

I don't like spiders. Sometimes I encounter them in the monastery and I've got to wrestle with the question of what I'm going to do with them. Sometimes we have situations where bees get into the monastery at certain times of the year. We trap them with cups and take them outside. We yell at them, "Don't come back!" They always come back. Bees know something about spiritual life. What wonderful teachers bees and all insects can be. So when we say not to kill other beings, there's something bigger here other than just the decision, "I'm not going to eat meat anymore."

The second practice of virtue is not to steal. We all know what happens when people steal. But we're not just talking about the stealing of things. You can steal time from someone. Do you really need to talk to me today? There was a psychiatrist that I used to meet at one point in my life. I remember in the beginning feeling as if he really needed to be there every time I called. There were times when he said, "No, I can't see you right now. I have certain hours." And I thought, "What do you mean you can't see me right now? We've got to talk! I have this feeling right now that I need to talk about." And he would say, "No. I have another patient right now." I had wrestle with that feeling. Do we steal time from people? Do we steal energy from people?

So, stealing is much more than just taking things from people. Again, you have to wrestle with this. You've got to know when to bug people for their time and when not to. It's not an absolute proposition. You can't just say, "I'm going to be a vegetarian and I'm never going to call the Roshi." If you do that, then I'm going to call you one night and say, "Let's have a hamburger and spend the evening together." I love hamburgers. The ego mind thinks, "What did he just say? He loves hamburgers! He can't be a Buddha! Buddhas don't eat hamburgers!" If His Holiness the Dalai Lama did not eat meat in Tibet, he and his nation would have starved. Their prime source of food was yaks. You can't farm very well in Tibet.

A third practice of virtue is not to speak falsely. This involves intentionally trying to deceive someone. We need to look at our list of excuses. This is how we deceive ourselves and others, with our excuses. It involves gossip, even positive gossip. It involves slander.

A fourth practice of virtue relates to the misuse of sexuality. What does this mean to a Buddhist? It means whether or not we use sexuality just to get what we want. Is our sexual activity about our gratification or is it the celebration of real love and appreciation between two people? Do not use another human being for your own gratification. Sexuality is one way of communicating the Dharma. What is this Dharma? It is affirming that the beloved is precious, is valuable, is a Buddha. We celebrate that appreciation in our sexuality.

A fifth practice involves not misusing drugs and alcohol. Once a year in many Japanese monasteries, the Roshi and his students go to a local bar. All of the students get drunk on sake. They must. They must get drunk to the point where they are falling-down. They do this once a year. In this light, what do we mean by the misuse of alcohol and drugs? When the students fall, they must still be mindful of the shoji screens. If they fall through a screen, the Roshi is going to kick their asses when they get back. You can fall down as long as you don't harm yourself or others. Roshis are masters of failing and falling without harming themselves or others. Once again, there is no absolute rule. There is a time for getting drunk and there is a time for refraining from getting drunk. If you find yourself depending upon drugs or alcohol for some kind of transforming experience rather than your own nature, then you've got a problem.

The practice of not killing other beings, not stealing, not speaking falsely, not misusing sexuality and not abusing alcohol or drugs is what Buddhism refers to as the five trainings of the heart. This is fundamental spiritual life. It's fundamental humanity. The next level of a virtuous life is not just passively practicing these virtues, but cultivating compassion in the world. How many of us have had the experience in school of seeing a crowd of children taunting the class nerd. Maybe it was you. It was me at one time. I also remember wanting to step out and help the poor kid. Where did that come from? This innate quality is in you already. I once had a yellow Labrador retriever named Aubrey. Whenever she heard me get loud, she sat next to me and whimpered to make sure I was all right. We respond to suffering. If you're not responding to suffering, you are drugged with yourself. Compassion is inherent in us. This was the first realization of the Buddha, that who we are is compassion. If you aren't cultivating compassion in your life, you are not being who you are and suffering will ensue. I'm not talking about risk-free, convenient compassion. I'm talking about stepping out of a crowd and defending someone. I'm talking about refusing to countenance faggot or nigger jokes at the next family gathering. You might have to leave and never go to another family gathering. I did.

Why do we think about people like Mother Theresa, Shakyamuni Buddha, Jesus? Why do people like this come into our minds? Because they engaged life. They walked the walk. We usually just talk the talk. When

101

we walk the walk, we find ourselves saying, "No, we will not condone this with our silence, we will not condone this through indifference, we will not condone this through passive participation." I love you dearly mother and father; I love you dearly my friend, but we will not have this conversation. Here's where you need to be careful. Conquering the Romans makes you no different than they. Be careful. Don't make people wrong in the process of disapproving their behavior. How can we do this? You've got to find out. The moment we make people wrong on account of their ignorance, and that's all it is, you're no different than they are.

The Flower of Virtue

How do we cultivate compassion for all beings, including people such as Hitler? We can't exclude anyone from the embrace of our compassion. How do we do this? You have to start by engaging life.

You start by participating in the suffering of life. Those of you who pursue only comfort and convenience are never going to experience your Buddha nature. You've got to get into the game. It doesn't matter what the rest of the world is doing. This is not about changing the people who are causing the suffering; it is about changing the cause of suffering. Do you want to look for the cause of suffering in the world? Look right where you are. Refuse to engage in thoughts, to engage in talk, to engage in actions that harm other beings. Be virtuous.

In the practice of virtue, the precept of not killing expresses a reverence for all life. It becomes a reverence for all life, including one's enemy. Love your enemies. Bless those who curse you and pray for those who spitefully use and abuse you. Bow in the reverent belief that your enemy is the avatar of Buddha. This is the way of the Bodhisattva. Not stealing becomes a respect for others' labor. It becomes a respect for another's plight. It becomes a real awareness that we are all in the same boat. Even the rich. Can you imagine what they've got to go through to keep all of that wealth? Can you imagine how lonely they are? We only see what the cameras show us. The practice of virtue also requires us to understand fear. The guy who just broke into a jewelry store is very afraid. He's so afraid that he's got to hurt somebody. Can you honestly say that you've never thought of hurting anyone? I have.

The virtuous heart is an open heart. I, the Bodhisattva, know only one way. I will not harm other beings through thoughts, words or deeds. Some things you must always be unable to bear. This is the virtuous heart. You don't have to protest in front of the White House. That's not necessary. What is necessary is to go home, for example, and look at yourself in relation to your beloved one. When we discuss the heart of renunciation, this will become clear.

Right speech, right sexuality, not abusing intoxicants -- what is this really all about? My speech should always heal, sew harmony, not harm or show shame or discord. In the practice of the virtuous heart, my words should be intended to awaken others to their Buddha nature. I remember one day, while surfing the net, I came upon this person who decided to share with people his manifesto of what a Buddha is. He described a person who never gets loud, a person who never feels, who is never surprised. I read this wondering if this is a statue he's talking about or a living being. Wisdom, as we will discuss later, provides for you the means to be loud when you need to be loud, but with right speech; to be quiet, and ultimately sometimes to just shut up and sit while someone cries and mourns. It's the best thing you can do. The ego wants to act. "Say something! Do something! Help them!" Wisdom allows for us to know that the best thing at times is to just shut up.

Right sexuality actually has to do with a love for life, a love for all life. I remember when the movie "Blade Runner" came out with Harrison Ford. He has to hunt down these part-human, part-robotic beings. The scene in the movie that just blew me away is when he's on the top of a skyscraper fighting with the last robot and he finds himself hanging off the side of the skyscraper. All of a sudden, to his absolute bafflement, as he's about to plunge to his death, the very person he was there to kill reaches down and saves him. After this scene Harrison Ford reflects on this and wonders what made the robot save him. Maybe it was just a love for life, any life, just life. There is an experience awaiting your arrival, one that you may have glimpsed. Until you've had this experience, you are all the poorer for it. You see, most of us have an excitement about particular lives: him, her, and me. We have no idea about life, this energy that we call life, the reverence for it, the experience of it, the celebration of it, and the protection of it. Viewed in this way, the practice of right sexuality becomes a dance with life.

Some of you can begin the practice of a virtuous heart by going home, taking care of yourself, and doing the things that you think you are too busy to do. Go home and respect your life. Strictly speaking this is not your life. If it were yours, it could never be taken from you. Life is not what it seems to be. If it were your life, then you could stop death. We have to move away from "our" lives to life, to the sacredness of life itself. I remember driving down Route 29 from New Hope one morning at about 2 AM when I came upon a landscaping supply store. It was all lit up. I saw a strange rock and had to pull over to the side of the road to see if what I was seeing were true. Out of the middle of this rock, right through it, a pine tree was growing. I remember thinking that life is not about me; it's not about a pine tree. It's about life finding a way. I fell to my knees and brought my hands together in gassho, knowing that I was before God.

Go to a hospital where crack babies are born and watch them fighting with everything they have to stay alive. You've got to hold someone, as I've had the occasion to do time and time again, as they breathe their last breath. Most of you have never even breathed a breath like that in all your years of meditation. Talk to an emphysema patient about breath. Talk to a terminally ill person about life. Do you want to know what life is? Talk to them.

The virtuous heart reveres all life. The Bodhisattva seeks that which nourishes the spirit. It is our source. We need to be nourishing the part of us that creates life. We're not doing that. We need to express virtue wherever we go, demonstrate it in our own actions, our own words, and our own practice. If you live with people who don't understand what you're doing, then you need to get over it. Maybe the best thing you have to offer them is your practice. Stop trying to convert them to Buddhism and just practice. They'll get it. They may never tell you, but they'll get it. They know what you're doing. If they didn't know what you were doing, they would throw you out. They know what you are doing. It may just take them a lifetime to say it.

There is something else that you need to know about virtue. You need to know where it comes from. Virtue is not something you can imitate. You can't just "do" it. It is inherent. Don't take my word for it. You would not be reading this if you were not a virtuous person. How many times have you been aware of your own longing? Longing is the virtuous heart hungering to know God. The cave man who walked out one night and looked up at the moon and the stars and marveled at the heavens longed to understand the mystery. But we must not just understand it. We must enter it. Why do you think that people make billions of dollars from Star Trek movies? They know that you, like them, long for this mystery. We hunger for Nirvana. We hunger for God. What we don't do is cultivate the hunger. Jesus said blessed is he who hungers and thirsts for this. They will know God. There is something about the hunger that we need to persist in cultivating. You aren't cultivating it through indifference; you aren't cultivating it through passive participation; and you aren't cultivating it through your limitations. Why do you think that people built churches and cathedrals in the Middle Ages? I don't know about you, but I don't care whether I'm in a Catholic Church or a Buddhist Temple. I walk into one of these buildings and something is clearly available to me that isn't available to me in the busyness of my life.

The second most difficult lesson to get across to Zen students is the absolute necessity to cultivate this longing, this hunger. We're not cultivating it with our "doing" and our "having." We must bring it more and more to the surface. Have you ever watched a baby exploring your home? They scream bloody murder when you try to stop them. Do you think that that's an act? Do you think that this is some kind of infantile conspiracy? Infants feel that hunger so deeply that to be deprived of it is painful. And we take it lightly, don't we. What you need to do the next time they scream is hold them and feel their hunger. Watch them when they reach for something and you pull it away. You need to watch that because if you don't you are lost.

The baby is longing to be what it is. Your true nature is God-like and what you want to be more than anything else is godly. You want to travel the universe. You want to go where no man has gone before, and yet you waste you time on activities that drag you down and away from what you long for more than anything else and that is to be Godlike. Why do you do that? The virtuous heart is always creating the opportunity to witness this miracle. In the long hours of sesshin, the only thing that can at all come close to getting you through is the remembrance of miracles -- the remembrance of little children grabbing statues off the shelf. For you the "statue" is money, it's your possessions. To them, the statue is nothing more than a metaphor for everything you want to know and don't have the guts to pursue. There's nothing pretentious about a baby. It doesn't have to pretend. It wants you to know something: "Get out of the way! Because if you don't, I'm going to scream, yell, poop -- whatever it takes to get you out of the way. I want to explore everything." You did too at one time. When did you forget?

My father likes to tell people a story about when my friend Ken and I decided that we wanted to know what hurricanes were like. We tied ourselves to a tree in back of our house when a hurricane came by. When my father, being the adult, got home, my mother said, "Your son is tied to the tree out back and I can't get him down! Go get him!" My father stormed outside and bellowed, "What the hell are you doing up there?" I knew no matter what I said, he wouldn't understand. He had forgotten the wonder. Some of you have forgotten it terribly. Do you know what you've forgotten more than anything else? The excitement of getting in trouble. You're so fixated on doing things right that it stinks. You won't even come out and play with me. You've got to do things right. So you call and check with somebody. "Uh, is this what the Roshi wants me to do?" You don't even want to play with me. The monks will tell you that if you want to be in a relationship with me, you'd better be willing to fight. I have no interest in being in a relationship with anyone who can't have a good fight. In the end, we will love each other; we will pick up the pieces. But if you can't fight, there's no possibility for you and me. You forgot the fun you had getting in trouble. You had fun. I had fun. You loved it. You knew you were going to get in trouble when you got home! And you still did it! Why? Are you stupid? No! There was something you once knew about the wonder, the joy of risking it!

Have we really forgotten that much? If we have, then we must realize that the practice of a virtuous heart is cultivating the opportunities to remember. What do we always say when stress gets really bad? "I've got to go find some peace and quiet." Why? What is it about silence and being still? Well, that's where you started, isn't it? Wasn't that what was going on in the womb? So what is spirituality? It's nothing more than meeting our life's longing, our deepest needs. We all want to return to the source. You don't have to wait to go home until you die. You can go home now. But you've got to go through the forest, and there are wolves in the forest. Ask Little Red Riding Hood. Some of you ought to be ashamed of yourselves when a little girl in a red hood can take on the wolves and you can't.

When you read those fables, you can see that they're no different from the great masters' stories. They're all telling you the same thing, aren't they? You don't have to go out and get a book on the laws of the universe! Buy a children's book and really read it. That's what some of you should be doing. God forbid that you walk around with a fairy-tale book! You've got to walk around with a big intellectual book on the teachings of the Buddha, such as the Dhammapada! But the one you run to is a little kid reading fairy tales. We all want to read them with him because we understood them when we were young and they understand them now. Do you know why your kids don't listen to you? Because they know that you don't know. They don't trust you. They saw that you sold out. That's why they don't trust you. You can't even be with them. You're so afraid of them that you've got to punish them when they don't behave properly. You've go to use brute power.

I will never forget living with my father, a man for whom I have nothing but the deepest respect and admiration. He was my first teacher, my first Zen master (not that I think he was trying to be that at all). I was the bad one in the house. You need to know that. One day, when I was grown, he said something that I'll never forget. "What I never told you was that I was always jealous of you. And I resented you for making me remember all that I had forgotten." He's now seventy and he's trying to get it all in as soon as he can. Do you want to wait until you're seventy?

The virtuous heart cultivates an environment conducive to remembrance. If you want to know how God feels, then start acting like God. Every thought, every word, and every deed is nothing more than the manifestation of that energy we call God. Otherwise, we manifest the opposite of that. All you have to do is practice right thought, right speech, right action. As master Dogen once wrote after years of teaching, if you want to be a Buddha, then simply care about other people. Simply refrain from harming other people. Engage people compassionately and they will say that a Buddha was born. What was Dogen pointing to? He was saying that the experience you long for is not hidden in some mysterious mountain or book; it is hidden in the practice itself. That destination for which you keep sitting, that object you keep waiting for to appear, will show up on its own. You will never "arrive" at it. This is the practice of satori. Enlightenment is zazen, is respect for all life, is cultivating compassion, is forgiveness. What does Jesus say to those who ask him, "Rabbi, how can I see the kingdom of God? Pick up your crosses and follow me." Pick up your excuses and follow me. Most of us understand that statement by Jesus to mean "believing" in him, but that's not what he was saying. What he was saying is that I had to suffer, so you've got to suffer. I had to forgive, so you've got to forgive. I had to go into the desert and meditate in order to help others, so you've got to go into the desert and meditate in order to help others. If you want to know what it is like to be Christ, then be Christ. If you want to know what it is like to be a Buddha, then be a Buddha. Throw the books away and stop looking for enlightenment everywhere else but right where you are. By being alive, you have been given the opportunity to do so. Wake up!

Ego-Mind, Fear, and Renunciation

I want to begin by reviewing the issue of context in order to be sure that you are clear about the power of context in our lives, particularly the context of ego-mind and fear. Contexts define what will show up in our lives. I want to be clear that they are not only the space in which things show up in our lives, but they literally determine what is <u>permitted</u> to show up. You can visualize contexts as the boxes in which we live. The box limits us. Those of us who are attached to our limitations clearly sense that our paradigm is powerful and constraining. Our boxes limit how far we can move in any given direction. They determine not only what we will feel, for example, but determine what we <u>can</u> feel.

We've all had the experience of trying to convince someone that we loved them and saying, "I just don't understand why he doesn't get it." The paradigm of his life might not permit him to get it. Our actions really are a function of our paradigm. Being late for an appointment is a prime example of this. When confronted about our failure to be on time, the mind refers to limitations. So, why are you late? Well, you know, Roshi, the traffic was bad; the weather was bad; the roads were icy, and so forth. These things may well be true and from your perspective that is why you are late. The egocentric mind and the paradigm of fear determine what you can even see. When you are asked why you are late, it rarely occurs to you that that part of the story is really just <u>part</u> of the story. The ego mind doesn't consider that if you left earlier you would have arrived on time.

Ego-mind limits our ability to consider alternate possibilities. In ego-mind, there are no alternatives. We always view life through the lens of impossibilities. "I couldn't because…" Our egocentric mind, this small mind, this paradigm of fear, functions exclusively out of limitations. It always views the world as a limited medium, not as an infinite set of possibilities. Jesus will not come back for you. We need to see the paradigm of fear for what it really is. Ego mind perceives itself within every angle of the box as limited because it functions from limitations. You start with limitations. You start with lack and this is why Buddha-mind cannot be perceived by the intellect. If you try this, egocentric mind will not let it happen. Buddha-mind transcends limited mind. It functions with an entirely different paradigm. It's impossible to understand it from the paradigm of fear. It's impossible. That is why it is so difficult for many students to achieve anything. They are always operating from limitations. That is the nature of ego mind. Limitations are the barometer of a situation's potential.

The Buddha says that life is suffering. Then he says that there is a source, a cause for our suffering. It's not as if there's nothing we can do about it. The source of our suffering is attachment to our limitations, to our attachment to ego-mind. In the ego-mind we perceive limitations. When you start with the experience of insufficiency, desire inevitably follows.

When I'm convinced that I can't do or have something, it follows that I desire it. How can I get it? What do I need to do? From the paradigm of lacking comes our desiring. Whenever I experience myself as lacking and limited and ineffectual, what always follows is a desire, a craving. It is our attachment to our limitations that gives birth to our desires. It is our attachment to our desires that gives birth to our reality. It is our attachment to our reality that gives birth to our illusions. It is our attachment to our illusions that deludes us. Thought made manifest forms words; words develop into deeds; deeds develop into habits; and habits harden into character. You are what you think. If you think you are limited, you are limited. What always shows up in the domain of limitations is suffering.

It would be nice if you could be limited and not suffer, but limitation is the context for suffering. When someone offers to do something for you and says the word "but," the conversation is over, because what always follows a "but" is a lie, is some excuse, is some limitation. Limitations are only perceptions; that's all they are. My limitations are my own. The truth of the matter is that I really could do something for you, but it will mean my making some sacrifice that I don't want to make. That's the truth. So tell the truth. I really don't want to do what it will take for me to do you a favor.

You think that you don't want to have to deal with your friend's hurt feelings. The truth is I don't want to have to tell them the truth so that I don't have to hurt <u>my</u> feelings. That's really the issue. I don't want that discomfort. I've got enough to deal with already. I don't need to deal with their feelings as well! If you are taking this as something bad, then your understanding is not deep enough. If you think that Buddhas don't have egos, then think again. Ego mind is an integral part of Buddha nature just like virtue is an illusion without non-virtue.

True spirituality involves risk. It involves a cost. In the Paramita of renunciation, we begin to be more aware of the power of all of this. Writing about Suzuki Roshi, Charlotte Joko Beck observes, "Suzuki Roshi said, 'Renunciation is not giving up the things of this world, but accepting that they go away. Everything is impermanent. Sooner or later everything goes away. Renunciation is a state of non-attachment, the acceptance that things go away. Impermanence is, in fact, just another name for perfection. Leaves fall, debris and garbage accumulate. Out of the debris comes flowers, greenery, things that we think are lovely. Destruction is necessary. A good forest fire is necessary. The way we interfere with forest fires may not be a good thing. Without destruction, there could be no new life and the wonder of life, the constant change could not be. We must live and die, and this process is perfection itself. All this change is not, however, what we had in mind. Our drive is not to appreciate the perfection of the universe, not to appreciate impermanence. Our personal drive is to find a way to endure in our unchanging glory forever. Who hasn't noticed the first grey hair and thought, oh-oh.'"

The moment gurus and Roshis mention renunciation, everyone immediately goes into a defensive posture. Everybody protects themselves, locks the bank, and sends out the soldiers. Our immediate thought about renunciation is, "Oh no! He's asking me to sell everything to the poor and now I have to go out and live in the streets with street people." The truth of the matter is that you can do that, but that is not the heart of renunciation. Life is not what it seems to be. Renunciation has to do with not possessing, not owning, not wanting, not attaching. It is our possessing, our owning, our saying, "Mine, mine!" that causes problems. It comes to all of us. We will hear, "Mine!" It becomes about possessing. It is our possessing, our owning of things, our wanting, our craving, our desiring and our attachment to things and people and feelings and ideas and beliefs that cause suffering. Our attachment to these things points to wrong understanding. But there is wonder in the miracle of change. Somehow life manages to make its point.

Things are not yours. They don't belong to you. They're not here to live your story. They may participate in it if they so choose, but all that energy we put into trying to keep them and our environment the same is the function of a deluded mind.

Renunciation is viewing the universe exactly as it is. Upon the attack of the tiger, the Christian martyr in the Coliseum said, "Oh the joy of letting go." The joy of letting go. As John the Baptist said, "Cut off my head." The joy of letting go. We have been fooled by our doing and having. The paradigm of fear deludes us. When people say, "Come to my house," very few of them really mean it. You know that when you buy a house, you end up having a thirty-year relationship with the bank. The house doesn't belong to you; it belongs to the bank. Don't make those payments and watch how long you get to stay there. After you pay for the house, the termites move in. After you get the termites out, the house burns down. Eventually you die. What can you say is truly yours?

There is something that is mine. It's the only thing that really belongs to me. When we talk about objects and people, nothing is "mine." The practice of renunciation is the acknowledgement that I and everything I own will one day pass away. Jesus said to his disciples, "All things will pass away, but my word will not pass away." Jesus was saying what the Buddha said five hundred years before. The Buddha said that my body is of the nature of impermanence. It will get sick and it will die. Everything I own is of the nature of impermanence. It will decay. It will go away. The people in my life are impermanent. They will go away, even if it isn't until they die. However, my actions are mine. They are the ground of my being. The only thing that really is mine is my actions, my lifestyle, my code of living. Renunciation is embracing the truth. It is viewing and operating in the world according to its reality. What is that reality? Everything is impermanent. It's not yours; it doesn't belong to you; you just have it for a little while, even if you have a receipt.

The practice of renunciation is about seeing what's really there. All of this mind stuff is not really there. It does not exist. If you want to experience joy and fulfillment and love and satisfaction, then the first thing you need to renounce is this idea of me, myself, and I. You know, "Me, Myself, and I", the holy trinity. God told you to forgive, to renounce grudges, past hurts, whatever. You know, God the Son, God the Father, and God the Holy Spirit -- that other holy trinity -- told you to forgive. If you say, "But I'm not going to!" then it must be the former trinity that you're worshipping. That is the holy trinity for most people.

In training the mind to open to the heart of renunciation, the easiest place to start is by renouncing things. We have to let go of possessing the material things in our lives. Mother Theresa once said, "If you find yourself in the streets of Calcutta, be in the streets of Calcutta. If you find yourself in a palace, be in the palace." Don't be in the streets trying to be in the palace and don't be in the palace trying to be in the streets. It's not about going home and selling all of your possessions so that you can feed the poor. It's about letting go of your attachment to things. How many of your fights are about money, about things? "I want a new car!" So we can't be having fun and eating out and making love in the meantime so that you can get a new car. This is more than a little absurd, but that is how many of us live.

There's a wonderful story about a town many years ago that had a great Holy Man in it. The town was hit by a flood and the tax collector managed to get himself stranded on a rock in the middle of the flood. The townspeople ran to him shouting, "Give us your hand! Give us your hand!" The tax collector kept clinging to the rock and wouldn't let go. So the townspeople ran to the Holy Man and told him that the tax collector was stuck in the middle of the flood and was going to die! The Holy Man agreed to help. He went outside and saw the townspeople yelling, "Give us your hand!" Nothing was happening. The Holy Man climbed onto the stone nearest the tax collector and said, "Here, take my hand." The tax collector grabbed his hand and was brought to shore. On the way into town the Holy Man turned to the townspeople and said, "Never ask the tax collector to give you anything." That's how most of us live. We'll go to our graves clinging to what we think is ours and we will drown.

"Before you act, think of the poorest person you have ever met and ask yourself if what you are about to do will benefit and will help them," said Mahatma Gandhi. You find this written at his memorial site in India. Those were his final words to the world. When we talk about renunciation, we talk about right effort. Our stuff does not belong to us anyway. Stop working so hard to have it and keep it. You don't need much. When I was traveling in Southeast Asia, I watched families singing at night and dancing and smiling who lived in huts with no furniture. How could that be? We really don't need that much stuff. Renunciation of the possession of others is the second part of our training. It's not just the possession of stuff; it's the possession of others which often translates to control. We need to take a look at how much of our life is about controlling others.

Psychotherapists recognize two types of personalities: the passive aggressive and the aggressive. Aggressive people control others through intimidation;

passive aggressive people control their environments through their limitations. How many of us control our environments with our limitations? How many of us have learned to do that? The paradigm of fear taught you that. We all learned somewhere in our life to control our environment with our limitations. One of the first times I can remember doing it is when I had to take tests in school. Every time I knew that there was a test coming, I got sick the night before. Even our illnesses can be a learned experience to control our environment. How many of us will be sick no matter what we do? We have learned to control others with our sickness.

The heart of renunciation simply begins by giving up possession of things, giving up control of our environment and others. You have got to find out how you are controlling, how you are possessing people in your life. How do you do that? Are you aggressive? Are you passive aggressive? That is the question you need to answer. There are two ways in which we control people. The first is by grasping. "Mine!" "I expect you to be this way or else…," and the big one, "If you really love me…." We always use love. It's like when I was a kid, and God bless them, I mean no judgment by this, but my parents were always fighting. I remember one time thinking to myself, "Oh yeah, I really want to get married!" How many of us have caused others to not trust in love because we use it on them: "If you loved me you would…"

Another way we control our environment is through aversion. We love to complain. Take a look at your relationships. How much time do you or your friends spend complaining? Your complaints or their complaints. I want you to know that if you're not doing the complaining but they are, it involves you anyway. It's no accident that you're with them. If you really don't want to do this, then get out of the relationship.

Two other ways in which we try to control people and things is by grasping or through aversion. We love to complain and we love to hold grudges. We love having grudges because as long as we have them, we don't have to participate in the relationship. In the paradigm of fear, the ego mind does not allow you to know that you can have a grievance. There are real grievances. But how many of us immediately think that moment we have a grievance, everything else stops? The love stops, the sex stops, it all stops until you address my grievance! How many of us consider the possibility that we could have a grievance and still respect each other, still celebrate each other and handle the grievance. That's what the Japanese have over American businesses. In American business, if the employees have a grievance, they shut down the business while the Japanese keep on producing. They continue working and they negotiate. They talk with mutual respect for one another.

How many of us love to hold a grudge? Grudges are our license to not participate in relationships constructively. Let go. How long can you be mad and think it matters?

The final training of renunciation has to do with renunciation of fear. This completes the practice of renunciation. How can I renounce fear? The renunciation of fear is choosing not to be managed by it. One of Jesus' disciples walked up to him one day and said, "You know, Jesus, we don't have to go to Jerusalem. If you go to Jerusalem, you will be crucified." What was Jesus' response? It was as if he knew from the beginning that he was destined to be crucified. The ego-mind does not allow us to consider that we can be scared to death and still act with integrity, still act with devotion, still act with loving-kindness. Isn't that what our heroes are? They are the people who are terrified by the prospect of running into a burning building, yet they still do it. We think that heroes are people who are not afraid of anything. Why renounce fear?

Because it does not exist. Fear is a lie. Fear is a story. "If I go in that burning building I will die!" If you don't go in that burning building you will eventually die anyway. Everything is changing. What are you holding onto? "My life." Your life? Your life is not yours to hold onto. Fear is the story we tell ourselves. When does it show up? When anything I do or say threatens what I want or expect. "If I go into that burning building, I will die." Where is the fear in this? Is the fear in the building? Is it next to you? No. It's in the story you're telling yourself about the thing. Fear is never in the object of fear, is it? Do you think that people who run into burning buildings while thinking about their fear will be effective? They might as well stay outside. Fear is in the story that you tell yourself.

We also need to look at how much we are attached to fear. We love it. For some of us it is the only time we know we are alive. But fear is a lie. It is a story we tell ourselves. So we just give it up. We renounce it. We renounce fear as managing our lives. So I feel fearful. So what? You can say to yourself, "What did I think I was going to feel? That's an awfully big fire." Renounce fear and you can get beyond it. There's more going on here than the fire. Someone is trapped and will die unless you renounce your fear and intervene.

Renunciation does not have to entail literal poverty. It's not about going home and selling all of your possessions to feed the poor. It's about being open to the eventual loss of your possessions. If nothing else, you will lose your possessions when you die. If you lose them before that time, can you be okay about it? True freedom is the activity of letting go.

In order to practice letting go, you must become aware of what you are holding onto. Reflect on what it is that you will not let go of. What is it you are holding onto? Whatever it is, let go of it. That is your practice. Let go of whatever it is: an idea, a feeling, a grudge, an image. What do you need to let go of in order for your life to move on? What is it that you keep holding onto that prevents you from living fully?

Renunciation is accepting the impermanence of all things. Renunciation is nothing more than acknowledging that things will not last. In that domain, how do you think life begins to be lived? What do you think is almost immediately generated by your choice to practice the heart of renunciation? Look at a baby prior to its being perverted. We know what is natural and true at a deep and vaguely remembered level. How do we get back to that, how do we bring it back to the surface? By practicing the heart of renunciation.

Wise Effort, Effortless Wisdom

Along with the heart of renunciation we need to practice wise effort. The Buddha is wise. The Buddha doesn't impulsively run into a burning building. The Buddha knows what he is doing every step of the way. This is wise effort. This is right effort. When we talk about wise effort we are actually talking about vitality. We are talking about right energy, the energy you put into something. Some of you are tired in your Zen practice because you are practicing with wrong effort. You are practicing with the wrong energy.

When we talk about wise effort, we are talking about acting in relationship with life as it really is. The question that arises naturally is, "What is the wise use of energy in the spiritual life?" Why do we ask the question that way? How do we use this energy in spiritual life? Why do we ask the question?

It's because we are spirit. What are you if you are not spirit? Here today. Gone tomorrow. What is that if not spirit? It's not like a psychic connection that allows you to call you grandmother from the other side. What are you if you are not spirit? What is the wise use of this spiritual energy?

To this end, the Buddha was asked, "What is Buddhism?" He said, "If you find something that works, do it. If you find something that doesn't work, don't do it." But we persist in doing things with very little mindful attention to what we are doing and with very little concern for the consequences of our actions. Most people do not appreciate the impermanence of their bodies until they have a cardiac arrest or something similarly catastrophic. Then all of a sudden, everything is about living. All of a sudden the choice to slow down and smell the flowers becomes imperative. It is stupid to wait until you have cardiac arrest. Why do you need a heart attack to understand that? Why do you have to be told you have a terminal illness to understand that? We need to live our lives by being mindfully attentive to the fact that the king has no clothes. You know that fairy tale? If you remember, it was a child who finally had the gumption to say, "Hey, he's naked!" You need to have that kind of courage. Spiritual life takes courage. You need to have the courage to say to yourself, "Who are you fooling?" To live otherwise does not cultivate the energy you need to awaken to your true nature.

Remember, we started out with the premise that you want to be a Buddha. If you don't want to be a Buddha, then you can go through life asleep. But to be a Buddha you have to go through life mindfully. You have to practice with wise effort, and wise effort is simply letting go of what does not cultivate the ground of awakening. Let go of the things in your life, the relationships in your life that harm either you or others. In turn, cultivate devotion in your life. Most people, I have learned, have no idea about the joy of labor. When Mother Theresa composed her constitution for her nuns, she used the word "labor" instead of "work." She didn't say work with the poor; she said labor with the poor. "Labor" means to work until you drop. It's not the kind of labor that most students put into their practice. "Well, I sat for fifteen minutes today. It was cool. It felt good." Of course it felt good, but that's not the point. It doesn't matter how you feel. That's another delusion of our age.

Suzuki Roshi used to have his students come and visit him. They often related visions to him. "I saw these lights...and they transformed into this figure...and this person came to me..." He would listen to them and when they were all done he would say, "Don't worry, it will pass." He didn't intend to invalidate the experience at all. He wanted to help the student realize that visions were not what the practice is about. Do you know how many people in the world are having visions? What changes the world is your participation in life as it is. Life itself is a vision. From a tiny egg, you emerged! What other vision do you need?

We need to move from good and bad, right and wrong to wise and skillful. Some of you will never practice skillfully because you practice with the intention of doing it "right." You practice with doing it the way the Roshi says to do it, not with the intention to awaken, not with the intention to be like a Buddha, not to be like God. That's probably because you have no idea what God is like because you've never really looked at anything God did. I have. It's beautiful, phenomenal. Clean your part of the monastery that way!

Sit that way and watch what happens. Listen to your child the next time that way! Go home and listen to them with the absolute devoted intention to hear what they are saying, not to tell them what to do.

We have to move away from our fear of practicing "wrong." Most students misunderstand me when I say that. They think that they have the license to practice any way they want. No you don't! You do it wrong and I'm going to hit you! You do it wrong and I'm going to let you know you did it wrong. So what do I mean? What I mean is that there is something bigger than your doing it "right" rather than your doing it "wrong." Practice has nothing to do with it. I don't care if you do it "right." What I do care about is that you practice skillfully because that is what a Buddha does. Do things in the same spirit that Michelangelo painted the ceiling of the Sistine Chapel -- skillfully and creatively. We must cultivate wise and skillful effort.

Effort in spiritual practice is not about doing and having. Doing it "right" as opposed to doing it "wrong" comes from the domain of doing and having because you will notice that what is motivating you to practice "right" is your fear of doing it "wrong." That's the paradigm of fear. Neither is it about a goal or objective. In The Agony and the Ecstasy, in which Charlton Heston played Michelangelo, the Pope came into the Sistine Chapel and asked him, "When will you be done?" Michelangelo replied, "When I make an end of it." The Pope persisted. "When will you make an end of it?" Michelangelo retorted, "When I'm done." They went on in this way until the Pope gave up and let Michelangelo work unmolested. He wasn't interested in "finishing" the ceiling. Why? He understood that the passion and the joy are in the process of creation. That's what many students never understand. Your eye is on an imaginary objective and you are missing the process. It's right here and right now. It's in the sweating, it's in the discomfort, it's in being with the process. That is what we call wise energy. Energy doesn't concern itself with good or bad -- it concerns itself with manifesting.

Wise effort is to live fully. To live fully is to be present to what is, exactly as it is. Our practice, when effective, is to be present to what is going on. If I'm coming down on you, be present to that. If I'm expressing gratitude, be present to that. If your sitting is blissful, be present to that, but when it's done, let it go. It will pass. If your sitting is difficult, be present to that. It will pass. Life doesn't care about your idiosyncrasies. You need to be present to that aspect of life. That's what makes it wonderful. The most powerful spiritual story ever written is the story of Job. This story says it all. Job goes through no end of misfortune and at the end he wants to know the mystery behind it all. And God replies, "Where were you when I created the universe?

What makes you think I should tell you the secret?" Can you be loyal in the face of that abyss of unknowing?

Until we open ourselves to the benign indifference of life, we can't really appreciate the energy of wise effort and how it can enliven us. Jelaluddin Rumi says that what the child needs is the stick of the father and not the gentle hand of the grandmother because when the grandmother dies and the father dies, the child will rely on himself, which is as it should be. We need to teach our children to deal with life instead allowing them to run home and hide. We need to take a look at how we set our kids up for great disappointment in our efforts to protect them from those parts of life that we don't want them to see. The Buddha's father paid for that. He spent twenty-some years hiding suffering from his son, as if that would keep him around. He learned the hard way.

There's a wonderful, true story about a golfer from Argentina who had won many tournaments. After winning this one tournament, he encounters a very poor woman who accosted him and told him that her child was sick and that she had no money to get medicine for him. The golfer is moved by this woman and he says, "Here take my winnings." When he goes back inside the club, a friend says, "Did you just give that woman all of the money you won?" The golfer said yes. He explained that she was afraid that if she did not get some money, her baby would die. His friend told him that he'd been conned. This woman goes after everybody for money and she doesn't even have a baby. The golfer's response to his friend was, "You mean the baby won't die this week? Well, that's the most wonderful thing I've heard!" He just let it go. Be present to life as life is.

The quality of a spiritual life is determined by your willingness to practice it as an adventure. Sadly, we start testing things, looking around the next corner. What's in it for me? What's the cost before I decide? Should I do O-Rohatsu this year? How long do you think the Roshi will make us sit? Did he make you stay up all night last year? We start bargaining with life. Get over it! Can't you just die? Just jump in. You might fly. Spiritual life is exploring and taking whatever you get. Why can't you just take what you get? "All day I sat in sesshin and you'd think I would have woken up and all I got was a sore ass!" Do you think that sore asses have nothing to do with being spiritual? If you could take the sore ass now and be content with it, you will find out what freedom is. The truly free person is not the person who knows how to manipulate life so that there is no sore ass.

Yes, practice can be painful, but you will find out that there is a domain of being where you can be with pain and still persist in your efforts to be free.

This certainly does not mean that you go out of your way to create more pain. The Buddha was against ascetic practices. To be with life no matter what it brings us is wise effort. The practice is not to avoid pain, but to learn how to live with it.

The ego says that we have to be careful. "This guy may not know what he's talking about!" You're limited; you only can do so much. That's how the paradigm of fear works. The paradigm of fear is always reminding us, "Psst... watch out." But it is our nature to seek, to explore. It is who we are. We want to explore. Most of us are suffering in our practice because we are holding back. We are not risking anything. But by nature, we want to risk. We want to remember what it was like to take risks like we did when we were young. Our freedom is in the reunion with the person we were as children. "Unless you become like a little child." What do you think Jesus was talking about?

Someone came to me years ago for counseling. She was having problems in her marriage and she said to me, "I'm going to go to a Cistercian Monastery so that I can learn to be patient." I said, "What are you going there for? You've got the best monastery in the world: your husband. Go home to him. I can't think of anywhere else to learn to be patient than with him." The moral of the story is that we have our practice right in front of us and most of us suffer with the idea of practice because we don't want to practice. In the same way that the bell rings for us to queue up and go into the Zendo, life is constantly giving us our cues. Whatever is going on in your life is your practice. So if you ask me what to do, my answer is, "What is going on?"

If you ask me what to do to be free, I will tell you to do whatever you are most afraid of doing. You need to find out what that is. You will never be free until you confront your demon and wrestle it to the ground. In the front of Japanese Zen monasteries, there are always two statues of demons. You have to get past those demons in order to enter the Monastery. Your practice is to confront your demons, to ask and to answer the questions that you don't want to ask, to look at what you don't want to look at. That is your spiritual practice. Wise effort understands that life is presenting us with cues all the time.

How does Zen offer us an opportunity for this kind of practice? Foremost is the practice of seated meditation. In proper seated meditation, we are given the opportunity to look at our relationship with the demons. What is our relationship with discomfort? Are you only kind and loving when you feel good? Is it possible for you to consider the possibility that you can be sick and kind and gentle at the same time? People do it every day. Parents the world over are doing it right now, working three jobs and then waking up at three o'clock in the morning the feed the baby. It's possible. And if it is possible, then what does that say about you? Are you willing to make that kind of commitment?

Whatever it is that keeps you from being compassionate and loving is your demon. Zazen gives us an opportunity to find that demon because seated meditation is a microcosm of our life, especially during sesshin. That is why I love sesshin more than anything else. It makes us confront the demons. They show up in sesshin. Another technique used in Zen Buddhism is the student-teacher relationship. Beware of the teacher who promises you bliss. In the practice of real spirituality, the teacher functions as a mirror. Nothing else. If she is a good teacher, if he is a wise teacher, all they do is show you what you look like.

Last, but not least, the other instrument used in Zen Buddhism is the Sangha. The Buddha was clear that relationship is the battleground for freedom. Those of you who spend your lives avoiding <u>being</u> in your relationships had better wake up. There's a reason why you become annoyed at the things your partner says. Find out what it is because that's your demon. Wrestle it to the ground so that you can be free, until you can listen to what they say and it doesn't tear you apart. Life gives us what we need. Life finds a way.

Your life is not what it appears to be. You think it's about the years that you've been here, your birth and your death. It's about freedom as well. It's all about freedom and life will do whatever it has to do to provide us with the means for achieving it. So life brings annoying people to us; it brings loud teachers to us; it brings teachers who are relentless, who won't bargain with us, who won't play our games. Your children are no accident and your parents are no accident. Your job is no accident and your boss is no accident. You need to go to work and look forward to being with that pain-in-the ass boss of yours because he will liberate you. Practice being with him and giving your all to your job for the good of the people in the company and you will realize your freedom. You will find out that you don't need bosses to act in a certain way for you to act a certain way. That's what freedom is. They can take our lives, but they will never take our freedom. That's what freedom is.

Wise effort is letting go of grudges and recognizing them for what they really are -- wonderful opportunities for freedom. They have a lot to teach us. The greatest teachers in my life were my enemies. Thank God I have a lot of enemies. The Sufis say you aren't a good teacher until you have a thousand enemies. Otherwise, your teaching has no value. Only someone who has experienced difficulty can teach about it. How could they do otherwise?

The only way that you will appreciate your freedom is to go through the fire. Nothing will better change the obnoxious employer than to realize that he doesn't affect you anymore. If you keep telling him he's got power over you, then you're giving your power away.

To summarize, Zen, zazen, the teacher-student relationship, and the sangha are the three instruments used to transform the student. Transformation is a mystery. For most of us, the biggest problem in our practice is this "knowingness" attitude. It's all mystery. A famous Korean Zen master used to teach his students about "don't know mind." He would ask his students, "What is the essence of Buddhism?" and his students would say, "I don't know." He asked, "Why did Bodhidharma come to the west?" "I don't know." He then asked, "What is the meaning of Zen?" "I don't know." And finally he would say, "Very good. Keep practicing 'Don't know mind'." Let go of your conclusions. They are blocking you. You have no idea. I don't care who told you what happens after death -- no one knows. You'll find out when you die. It's all a mystery.

True spiritual practice provides us with the context to face our fears and discover our courage. Right effort is risky. Right effort is also balanced. We talked about this earlier. The Buddha taught, "Tie it too tight, it will break. Tie it too loose, it will not play." Buddhism is the Middle Way. Some of you need to create more balance in your life. Too much "I can't" or too much "I can do all of it" is unbalanced. There's a middle ground here that you've got to find. I can't tell you how to do it. You need to sleep when you are sleepy, eat when you are hungry, exercise when it is time to exercise, to meditate, and learn. You must participate fully and purely in whatever you do. The Dalai Lama told his students that they must create a balance between meditation and learning -- all meditation, no learning; all learning, no meditation. So in zen monasteries you are told that everything is practice. That's the balance. Practice is not just doing, doing, doing. It's not how long you sit. We can go up into the zendo and sit for five minutes and in five minutes you can become a Buddha if you know how. It's not the content; it's not the length; it's the quality of your effort. This is wise effort.

Right effort is steadfast. You can't apply right effort until you renounce giving up. I remember years ago watching one of those talk shows and some famous actors were on the show. They all had something in common; they had all been divorced and remarried to the same person. After remarrying that person, their relationships were much stronger and went on for years and years. The host asked them, "How did you do it? What did you do differently the second time than the first time?" One of the couples answered that this time giving up was not an option. They renounced giving up. For some of you, your excuses will continue to show up in your life because you have created a space for them to show up. What is that space? Giving up. If you don't have the space for giving up, excuses disappear. They have no power over you. Excuses are only reasons for not doing something. Some of you need to create right effort as steadfastness. Not sitting today is not an option. Not practicing loving-kindness is not an option.

Right effort produces the energy of confidence, ease and wisdom. There is nothing more powerful to transform your spiritual practice than the context of steadfastness, of renouncing the option of giving up. There is nothing more powerful than knowing that the only option you have is to succeed.

I was giving workshops one year on the occasion of a blizzard. It was Saturday night and as we were leaving, one man raised his hand and said, "Will we still have the workshop tomorrow if it keeps snowing?" I said yes. He said that if it kept snowing he might not be able to make it. I told him that in that case he would not have the workshop, but that I would. Then I said "Before you go, I want you to consider something. I will have ten thousand dollars for you if you come tomorrow morning." He said he would definitely be there. The truth of the matter is that we have the potential at all times to achieve anything we want to. We can forgive. We can let go. We can do these things. We can realize our Buddha nature. It's all up to you.

The Way of a Buddha

The Paramita of Wisdom is the heart of Zen Buddhism. What is wisdom? When you get to the heart of anything you reach the depths of non-definition. For example, if you ask me why I love someone, I can't tell you. Wisdom is like that. You either know it or you don't. I will tell you how to arrive at wisdom, I will tell you about the practice of wisdom, but I will not tell you what it is. This is a Paramita that defies definition. We can talk about the practice of prajna or the way of wisdom. We can say that wisdom is the awareness of the perfection in each of us, of the universe as it is. When we say that someone is wise, we sense that he or she sees things that we can't see. Among other things, the wise individual can see the whole person in each of us. The unwise person says, "Oh he's just a fool and a failure." But the wise know that there is no such thing as failure. Success is really the only outcome. Failure is an illusion.

Wisdom is not knowledge. It is not information. What most people don't understand is that when you start showing off your so-called knowledge by telling everyone what you know, all you are doing is transmitting information that has been given to you by someone else. It's not even yours. All your knowledge is a collection of information. In this sense, you're nothing other that a data base. Wisdom is not like that. It's not what we know.

"Yeah, though I speak with the tongues of men and of angels but have not love, I am but a sounding brass and a tinkling symbol. Though I may have all knowledge of heaven and earth but have not love, I am nothing at all. Even though I may be able to prophesy, I am nothing at all. Even though I know what happens to me after death, if I have not love I am nothing at all."

The poem asks us, "What really matters?" The wise man knows what really matters. For me, one of the most powerful stories about wisdom has to do with the story about King Solomon, when two women come to him, each claiming that a baby is theirs. The "smart" guy would have convened a trial and gotten lawyers and all of that and we would have gone on for days and spent millions of dollars to find out which one is the mother. But the wise person cuts through all of that and comes right down to the heart of the matter. Solomon says "Draw your sword and cut the baby in half!" Right away the real mother is revealed. That is what wisdom is. Wisdom is like what Crosby Stills Nash and Young used to say, "If they told you, you would cry, so just look at them and sigh and know they love you."

The wise person knows that children absolutely love their parents and that parents absolutely love their children. It is a given no matter how distorted its expression becomes. The wise person knows how to cut through the crap, and always arrives at compassion and love. When you start unveiling the disguises of your life, you will end up at the same place that Shakyamuni Buddha did because you can't end up anywhere else. There is nowhere else but love and compassion. Success in these is the only option. For some of you, your only problem is that you are practicing as if it isn't. If you say, "Well, what if I do all of this and I find out that I'm not a Buddha?" then you're not getting it. That option doesn't exist.

When most people talk about wisdom, they talk about it as something they hear outside of themselves. That is one way that people receive wisdom. Some people arrive at wisdom through a process of inward reflection, by meditation, and they see something. But the highest form of prajna paramita has to do with living intuitively and that's the problem. You have suppressed your intuitive nature for a long time. The shovel that we will need to uncover that hasn't been made!

I had a couple of dear friends when I was growing up; in fact there was always a gang of us and we were all crazy. One day, we were up in my friend's bedroom. He brought out an air gun. I said, "Ooh, this should be fun. Let me see it!" I got hold of the air gun, pointed it at his feet, and said, "Dance!" He danced around while I shot bee-bees at his feet. He was amazing, dodging those bee-bees. I finally got him after a while and he had to go to the doctor to have the bee-bee removed from his toe, but for a while he was doing really well ... until he thought about the bee-bee. But we'll deal with that later. The point for now is that you will be amazed at what you can do when you renounce failure as an option. Most of us can't even imagine living life at that level. Most of us don't even want to go there. You've got to be awake. Parents, you've got to listen to your children when there is no energy left in you to listen anymore. For the lover, you've got to give up making youy beloved wrong even when he or she is wrong.

I often tell the story about a Life Seminar program that I conducted years ago. I was talking about renouncing fault finding. A beautiful old man who used to work for my father raised his hand and said, "One moment please. I want to point something out to you; I don't make my wife wrong, she *is* wrong!" Imagine living at a level where you choose <u>not</u> to make the other person wrong. Some of you can't even imagine it because; after all, you have the right to air your grievances, don't you? Some of us cannot even imagine giving that up, not allowing that to be a determining factor in our relationships. It's the wise person who says, "You can screw up royally; you can even hurt me at the deepest part of my being and I promise you, I will not harm you." That's what Mahatma Gandhi said. "I don't care what the British do; I will not harm a single soldier." But what if someone cheats me? He or she is liable to if you have to ask that question. They can only cheat you if you create that option for them. I don't mean that you manage and control people. If you do your job in loving, why would your partner look anywhere else for satisfaction? Why shoot for the moon if you can have the stars? Some of you do not love in that way. Some of you need to go home and give your all. "But what's in it for me?" And then you wonder why people betray you.

Intuitive living brings self-reliance. This is not living from the egocentric self that declares, "I don't need anybody." It is not that self. It is the Self that takes in the universe. Intuitive living is absolute trust that the universe lacks nothing. "Behold the birds in the air and the lilies of the field." It's like that . "But how do I know I can trust that?" If you have to ask that, then you don't know what trust is. You aren't talking about trust when you ask the question, "How can I trust them?" In that case, you're talking about bargains and guarantees. Step out of that and choose to trust, no matter the outcome. What is the nature of the universe? Impermanence, interconnectedness, karma.

If you trust the universe as karma, life begins to work and isn't all that difficult. What is karma? Karma is simple. Every thought, every word, every action produces a reaction. Every kind of energy produces a specific kind of responding energy. Act lovingly, act gently, act with compassion and you get a specific result. Act with manipulation and malice and contempt and you will get a specific result. Your thoughts are connected to your words. Your words are connected to your actions. Your actions are connected to your experience. When you tell me you're too tired, my only honest response to you is what are you doing to be too tired? Imagine the sun being too tired to come up tomorrow. Imagine the wind being too tired to blow through your part of the earth. Imagine the seasons being too tired to change. Why do we see ourselves as being apart from that?

Wisdom is simple and always present in the Now. Wisdom is not in the past or the future. It's always right now. It's not about beliefs; it's not about speculation; it's not about ideas. It's "cut the baby in half!" How could Solomon have done that? It took a tremendous trust in human nature for him to do that. Solomon wasn't only risking his kingship, he was risking another life! He would have lost everything if those women did not respond and that sword went through the baby. He was convinced absolutely that those women would prevent it from happening. Imagine that! That is the trust we are talking about! Did Solomon know that for sure? Absolutely not! How could he? How could he know what those women would have done? What if they were both psychotic? Now, would Solomon handle the situation the same way every time? Absolutely not! Wise people don't do that. It's not about absolutes that we can apply to every given situation. It's about doing what is necessary. It's not tit for tat. Wisdom responds to a given situation exactly as it is. You want to know what to do? All you have to do is muster up the courage to ask the question, "What is needed here?" Then do it.

If you find yourself run rampant by your feelings and thoughts and emotions, you need to sit more. You need to practice zazen. You need to quiet your mind. You need to discipline yourself. If you find that your body isn't responding with enough energy, you need to look at how you are living. Don't go to the doctor! You might eventually have to go to the doctor, but notice how your first response is to go to the doctor. Look at what you are doing and you will find that you are probably doing something with your body that you need to stop doing or that you need to be doing more of. You need to be stretching your body during long periods of meditation. You need to be stretching your body beforehand. There is a moral dimension to this energy -- meditation doesn't work after a day of raping and lying. Sesshin doesn't work for a person who comes to it after sitting in an office all day for five days and expects to sit comfortably in a cushion for twelve more hours. You need to stretch your body. You need to get sleep. Those of you who come to sesshin after staying up till midnight the night before want to ask me, "Do we have to start at five o'clock?" No, but do you have to stay up until midnight?

The wise man is unaffected by either praise or blame. The wise man knows that if you really want something, then you will do what is necessary to achieve it. You can really love someone even if he or she is unable to love you in return. There is another thing the wise man looks at. Your life is being run by a paradigm. So is theirs. Those of you who are getting into relationships that continually fail, shame on you. We base the decision of who we are going to spend the rest of our lives with on the basis of a brief, infatuated acquaintance. You wouldn't buy a car that way! The wise man asks, "Does this person have, as the paradigm of their life, the space to include me?" Eventually the Zen Master says to the very busy student, "Apparently you have no room for me. Goodbye." And that may be what it is. You've got no room for me or others in your life. You keep telling me, "Well, I've got all this other stuff to do and then I'll get to you." It doesn't work that way with Zen masters.

The wise man is at peace with the world. He is absolutely contented to not know and is always watching. A wise person is absolutely content not to arrive at conclusions and will wait, will watch, will learn. Students are my greatest teachers. That's why you find me watching them so often. Wisdom does not add or subtract -- it simply is what it is. "The wind cannot shake a mountain. Neither praise nor blame can affect the wise," says Shakyamuni Buddha.

How do we cultivate wisdom? Quite simply. If you are going to practice the way of the Buddha, you do what is necessary and nothing else. That's how you cultivate wisdom. You don't add to it and you don't subtract from it. You do what is necessary and nothing else. Enjoy your successes, but remember what the Zen Master said to his young postulant who had had a great insight going up a mountain. When the student said, "Oh, it is so beautiful and so wonderful!" the master kept silent. Finally the student said, "Master! What do you think? Isn't it beautiful?" The master turned to him and said, "Yes, but it is a shame you have to say so." Wisdom is like that. Don't add your story to it. Keep your ego out of bounds. Be aware of it because it is always going to be with you. Your ego is your shadow, and most of you are like a little kid trying to step on his shadow and getting upset that it keeps following him. You want it to go away. That's what Zen students think practice is. "One day my ego will go away." Your ego will go when you die! Keep it out of your relationships and things will work; they will flow. The only time water does not flow is when something is put in its path. What is put in the path of all of your relationships is <u>you</u>. You are blocking the flow. What makes practice difficult is always the student's ego.

Wisdom is a function of absolute trust in the true nature of the universe. Buddhism teaches that the true nature of the universe is that it is ever changing, unlimited and abundant. Whatever happens to me will happen and I can guarantee that after it happens, something else will happen. It doesn't end. There is no ending. Those of you who are afraid of ending need to stop worrying. There is no ending. There is only change. There is only becoming and the only reason why we don't want to change is because we don't want to do the work. Change takes work; change is painful. Wisdom is the absolute trust that long before I arrived the universe was doing quite well. I don't need to change it, manipulate it or demand that it take anything from itself and, long after I am gone, it will continue. Life went on before I showed up and it will go on without me. You will go on. One of the most powerful lessons I learned was that everything is fleeting and the moment you become attached to something, the only thing that stops changing is you.

You've got to visualize this journey like going down a river and as long as you let the water take you where it will, it will take you. You will go around the rocks, under the rocks, bounce against the shore…. The only thing that will stop you from going down the river is when you reach out and grab onto something. So if you want to go down the river, keep your arms in the boat. Life is a roller coaster ride. If you try to get off it before it stops, you know what happens. Keep you arms in and enjoy the ride. You don't have free will. You try free will in this life and you will die. Free will is getting off the roller coaster ride before it stops. It's not about me. It never has been.

The other Paramitas speak for themselves. Consider the Paramita of patience. For most of us, patience is very much like renunciation. The very idea of practicing patience provokes an internal, "Oh, God!" Everyone says that patience is a virtue and they're right; it is. It is one of the virtues of a Buddha. But like everything else in Buddhism we don't say, "Ok, I'm going to <u>try</u> to be patient with him." Patience requires an appreciation of the cost of impatience. You can see this with a simple exercise. Close your eyes. Notice that whenever you are in a hurry, everybody else is going too slowly. Every time you are just taking your time and coasting down the road, all the other cars are going too fast. It's all relative. For a moment, I want you to notice yourself hurrying to get somewhere. You haven't anticipated the amount of time you need to reach your destination and now you are rushing. Imagine the last time you did that. Notice how you feel in the process. Identify the cost. Open your eyes.

A wise teacher and student are like the creator of a good bottle of wine. You can put in all the right ingredients; you can get the best bottle for the wine. But if you aren't willing to wait for it to ferment properly, to give it the time it needs, it will become vinegar. Patience is the realization that some people will just not achieve understanding tomorrow. Some things in life only time can transform. If you've ever lost to death someone who is very dear to you, no matter what anyone tells you, only time will transform your grief. Some things are just like that. Patience is also the realization that whatever it is you are waiting for will come to you. If you are waiting for students to wake up, eventually they have to wake up. Why? Because everything changes.

No one can sleep forever. Everything is impermanent. Now, what makes you impatient? Look at it. What is directly connected to your impatience? What is your impatience a function of? If you look deeply enough, you will see that "I want it and I want it now!"

There is this "I" again. There you are, practicing renunciation and causing all kinds of suffering; there you are, practicing right effort and causing some more suffering. Impatience is a function of the "I" being around. Nature has no problem with an "I." You're going to drop a nuclear bomb on this forest? Okay. It will take it ten million years to recover, but it'll be back. No problem. Nature has no problem waiting because nature doesn't have an "I". There is no "I" in nature. If there were, the deer would be forming a labor union! Do you see the "I"? It doesn't exist. It only exists in your mind.

The difficulty with patience has to do with "I" and "I" being unwilling to let go of my expectations. So, how do we practice patience? Every time you are impatient then breathe in, breathe out, let go. It is better to walk away from a situation with your discomfort, sit with it and be quiet. If you've got something to say about it, you can say it, but don't expect to get what you want. One way to practice patience is to give up your attachment to your expectations. Now, I didn't say to have no expectations. I've got expectations. But give up your attachment to them. Some people will never fulfill your expectations. Mark Twain said, "When I was a young child, I couldn't get over how stupid my father was. When I became a young man I was amazed at how smart he had become." Wisdom comes only with age and patience.

When you are present to the moment, you have two practices: you can walk away with your discomfort and handle it or you can voice your expectations, but not be so attached to them. Why do this? Because the reality is that there is no need for impatience. I am sure that Shakyamuni Buddha had no interest in converting people to Buddhism. It doesn't matter whether you are a Buddhist or not. This is not about Buddhism. Some of the greatest leaders in the history of mankind knew that they would not see the fruits of patience in their lifetimes. The fool asks, "Why?" A Buddha asks, "Why not?" That is the difference between a Buddha and a fool. If there's no space for what you want right now, give it time. It will come. What always follows incapacity is capacity. What always follows suffering is joy. What always follows joy is sadness. The only people who are happy all the time are on drugs. The practice of patience requires courage.

The Paramita of Truthfulness does not necessarily have to do with telling true but hurtful things, although sometimes it is necessary. The Paramita of Truthfulness can involve your telling yourself hurtful things. Shakespeare said, "To thine own self be true." We have to renounce our attachment to our excuses in order to live truthfully. Truthfulness would have us say: I am not sitting everyday; I need to be sitting everyday, but I am not doing it. It does not have us say, "I wanted to sit yesterday but…" That is the story of excuses. That is what life is for most people! A story. The renunciation of our story is absolutely required in order to practice the Paramita of Truthfulness.

The Paramita of Truthfulness requires steadfast discipline. It requires surrender of the story. The Paramita of Truthfulness is just what it is. It is the practice of truthfulness. Stop giving excuses. Just tell the truth. The truth will set you free.

The Paramita of Dedication is what it says what it is. Some of you have not said, "I am dedicated unconditionally to the realization of my Buddha nature. I am dedicated to not harming other beings. I am dedicated to doing the work I need to do to unveil my true nature." Some of you are still playing with this. Dedication requires giving your all. How do you give your all? You just do it. For those of you who have difficulty understanding that, it is a reflection of your attachment to the excuses of your life. You have not yet created the context for dedication. You don't understand that everything is a function of a paradigm. You don't have the paradigm for dedication when you have excuses showing up in your life. You can't devote yourself. It is impossible to devote yourself. You will never realize your Buddha nature until you create a paradigm for dedication.

The Paramita of Loving Kindness is explained by the Buddha in the Metta Sutra, a collection of his sayings. It describes our practice. "This is what should be accomplished by one who is wise, by one who seeks good and has achieved peace: let one be devoted, upright and sincere, without pride, easily contented and joyous; let one not be submerged by the things of the world; let one not take upon oneself the burden of riches; let one's senses be controlled; let one be wise but not puffed up, and let one not desire great possessions even for one's family. Let one do nothing that is mean or that the wise would reprove."

The next part of the Metta Sutra provides the context for this practice, and is a problem for many of you. The challenge of this practice is simply stated: "May <u>all</u> beings be content. May all beings be joyous and live in safety?" The key word here is <u>all</u> beings. You see, if you practice for yourself only, then forget it. It won't work. The context for practice is the benefit of <u>all</u> beings. May all beings experience joy and the causes of joy, not just me. In my relationships, it is not about my gratification alone. It's about <u>our</u> peace, our joy. "All living beings, whether weak or small, in high or middle or low realms of existence, small or great, visible or invisible, near or far, born or to be born, may all beings be content." Why do you think the Buddha said it that way? He is saying that everyone can achieve this. There are no excuses for anybody.

"Let no one aim to deceive another, nor despise any being in any state; let none by anger or hatred wish harm to another. Even as a mother, at the risk of her own life, watches over and protects her children, so with a boundless mind should one cherish all living beings." The Buddha gives us a context here. What is that context? Responsibility. The context for true Zen practice is responsibility. This is your earth. You occupy it. Keep it clean. The causes of suffering can be and should be eliminated. Our practice is to realize that it is my responsibility to eliminate the causes of suffering in my life and in the lives of others. You can't do this until you understand that it is your birthright to realize your Buddha nature; but it is also your responsibility to realize your Buddha nature because you chose to be human this time around.

"Suffusing love over the entire world, above below and all around without limit, so let one cultivate an infinite good will toward the whole world. Standing or walking, sitting or lying down, during all one's waking hours, let one cherish the thought that this way of living is the best path in all the world." With these words, the Buddha provides us with another aspect of responsibility. You've got to believe in this with all your heart. If not, you are just wasting your time. You can't imitate compassion. You can't pretend.

Abandoning vague discussions have a clear vision. Buddhas always know where they are going. There is no room for "I don't know." We don't have to think about it. It came to me some time ago that maybe this is why not too many people are dedicated to waking up. Because when you wake up, when all the excuses are gone, there is no possibility to hide anymore. It's as if nobody ever, ever, ever lets me get away with anything. Ultimately, there's no possibility for that.

Freed from sense appetites, those who have refined themselves and achieved perfect expression will never again know rebirth in the cycle of suffering for ourselves and others. Love is not the sentimental thing that we think it is. It's not a feeling that you have for someone. It's the thoughts and the words and the actions that you cultivate in your relationships with others. It is engaged participation. It's not love until you engage the object of your love. Love happens when you are really involved in caring for another being, when you feel responsible for their safety and their well being and you want the very best for them. You're willing to even, and most especially, "lose the vote" for that to happen. Some of you will never understand love until you give up the vote. The vote is whatever is in it for you. Do you know why you don't like politicians? It is not because they are a uniquely different species apart from human beings, even though it appears that way, but because they remind you of what you don't like about yourself. When we are doing something in return for something else, we are politicians. When we are in a relationship only to be loved, we are politicians. That is why we can't stand them. They remind us of the worst part of ourselves: me, me, me, I, I, I. "Oh, yes, I will go and fight for you; give me your vote." When we talk about loving kindness we refer to assertive participation, not some sort of passive participation.

Last but not least of the Paramitas is the Paramita of Equanimity. What is equanimity? To live in equanimity is to hold everything in life in the same light. The difficulty in my practice is as equally valuable as the pleasures and joys of my practice. Both work together in harmony for the same result. Some of you will never achieve this because you don't understand that the very thing you have a problem with is working on your behalf. It is more than likely the very thing that will liberate you. The difficulty is what will liberate you. You will never know your fullest potential if you keep cutting off and discriminating in your practice. To act in equanimity is to treat all circumstances, all situations, all beings, whether they merit it or not according to your judgment, with compassion and loving kindness; it is to renounce harming any being. There are some people I'd really like to pop! It may be the best thing that could happen to them! It seems as if it could be the best thing that could happen for me, but I just renounce that. When difficult people come to your house, treat them as you would your best friend.

The Bedouins in the desert have a tradition of hospitality that goes way back. No matter who comes to their tents, they give them food and drink.

No matter whom they are. In the desert, people know how to act; people know how to take care of each other. You have to go to the desert. You've got to be thirsty and hungry. You've got to lose it all and find yourself in the desert before you can understand what this is. The next time you are convinced that anyone merits your anger, stop a moment. Think about what it will be like when they are gone forever and then act. That's all. When I want to lose it and really hurt the people I love, that is all I have to do. What will happen to them? What will happen to those things I love about them? Will they change if I do this? Certainly with children it happens that way. You can break a child in the same way you break a horse. You can ruin it for life. Some of you have had that happen to you.

As Gandhi suggested, the activity of equanimity is anticipating the consequences of your words or actions. Are they worth it? Will they bring benefit; will they heal; will they sow harmony; will they really produce the results you want? The wise man understands that sometimes the angriest person in the world is really just somebody who is afraid that they will never know love. Even that person, as the Metta Sutra suggests, must stop and ask, "Will my actions bring the kind of love I want to know?" Consider the Middle East. I know one thing. If you bomb my children, I am going to be mad at you for a long time; and I am going to tell the next generation of children to be mad at you for a long time and they are going to tell their children the same thing. Violence only begets violence in any shape or form. If you keep calling me "no good," I am going to believe you one day. If you keep telling me that I will never amount to anything, I will believe you one day. The practice of equanimity is the discipline of one's response. Even if I feel self-righteous, I must say to myself, "May all beings have joy and the causes of joy; may all be freed from sorrow and suffering and the causes of sorrow and suffering." All I do by expressing self-righteous indignation is to create the causes for more sorrow and suffering. As a Buddha, this is not my prerogative. In fact, Buddhas do not have rights. Buddhas don't need rights. I have no rights. If I get locked up for my teachings one day, then I deserve it. I have no rights. It's like Jesus. He knew what was going to happen to him when he went to Jerusalem. They may take my life, but they can never take my freedom. I don't need your rights and I certainly don't have the right to harm you just because I feel like it. I can harm you and I can explain it away as self defense, and sometimes we do have to defend ourselves, but it doesn't change the fact that we've taken a life.

We have to stop thinking about what is right and what is wrong and start looking at everything as karma. We have to start looking at everything with equanimity. We have to respond with equanimity. If you go home and start practicing equanimity tomorrow morning when you wake up and people are not acting the way you wished they would and you practice loving kindness and gentleness with them anyway, then you will be free. Equanimity is being able to say, "It doesn't matter what happens in the world; I am going to be this way." What more freedom is there than that? What more freedom is there than waking up in the morning and deliberately saying, "I will not harm another being." What are you waiting for? That is it. That is what you have been waiting for. That is real freedom. That is why the Buddha understood that we must sit and meditate. But, we must sit and meditate not just for fifteen minutes because it feels good. We must sit and meditate and confront the demons in our lives and we must prepare ourselves to practice this way. You don't just do this. You have to be it. Life is suffering and it is difficult to do this. That is why you must devote yourself to doing the things you have to do in order to achieve this. Will you fail? Of course you will fail. I do it at least once a lifetime. Will you succeed? Yes you will because failure is not an option here. Temporary blindness is all that really goes on. You must do the work.

In the end, practicing the Paramitas is the way of a Buddha, not the way to becoming a Buddha. As Dogen would say, if you practice innate generosity, virtuous heart, heart of renunciation, wise effort, wisdom, patience, truthfulness, dedication, loving kindness and equanimity, then people will say you are a Buddha. That is it. No, really, that's it.

The Mind

What is True Freedom?

When there is no understanding of how this human mind, this egocentric machine functions from moment to moment, dissatisfaction and fear continues to run us. Simply living your life doing what you should do or worried about what you should not do, will not suffice and has nothing to do with full self-expression and living an authentic life.

Lao Tzu once wrote these words, "Be content with what you have. Rejoice in the way things are. When you realize there is nothing lacking, the whole world belongs to you." It is my intention to present to you the means of achieving for yourself, in your lifetime, the singular and exclusive objective of Zen, or as I prefer to say it, of any genuine spiritual practice. When a religion is genuine, the singular objective and exclusive purpose is always freedom, freedom of the individual. There's a problem, especially in our modern society, whenever we talk about freedom. We have a distorted view of its meaning, of what it truly means to be free. Most of us have come to believe that freedom is a kind of right to do as we please, to say what we please, to come and go as we please.

There is something that I learned at a very young age. If you want your life to work, there is a very simple way of doing it. Go home and read the dictionary. Noah Webster was a very enlightened being. The definition of words is clear whenever you pick up Webster's dictionary. When we look at Webster's definition of the word freedom and the words related to freedom, here is what he says: "Freedom is the state of being free." When we define "to be free," we find: "Not determined by anything beyond its own nature of being." Webster defines freedom as: "Not determined by anything beyond its own nature of being." As we look at the process, of freeing oneself, Webster defines it this way: "To relieve or rid of what restrains, confines, restricts or embarrasses. To disentangle; clear."

When we look at Webster's definition of freedom, we can see that it has nothing to do with externals or the outer world, as we call it in Zen. Freedom is an internal matter and any genuine spiritual practice is about the internal, the inner world of being. We commonly view freedom as something happening outside us. "If only this would happen; if only she would be this way; if only the country would change that way; if only the government would be this way." There are many, many others ways in which we do this.

From the Buddhist perspective, freedom is a function of awakening to one's true nature. If you remember Webster's words, to be free means not to be determined by anything beyond its own nature of being. Twenty-five hundred years ago, the Buddha, before Webster, defined freedom in the same way. Freedom is a function of awakening to our true nature, our original nature, and to live our lives in harmony with that nature of being -- to be one with who we truly are.

Freedom is not about having beliefs. Webster defines "belief" in this way: "A state or habit of mind in which trust or confidence is placed by the being in some other person or thing." To believe means to "accept as genuine or real," means to "fix the limits of." To believe in something means to surrender your authority over to another person or thing. Zen is not interested in beliefs. Zen is not interested in my beliefs. Zen is not interested in your beliefs.

Any genuine spiritual practice has facts for its reference. Spiritual practice is about what can be seen and what can be heard, not only with our sense organs, but also with the eternal eye or as we say in Zen, kokoro, the heart within. Zen is interested only in what can be seen when we take the time to actually look. Jesus once said to his students, "You have eyes to see, you have ears to hear, yet you neither see nor hear." Obviously he was pointing, as the Buddha was, to something other than just the physical eyes in our bodies. To actually see something face-to-face is to have the full experience of that something. These teachers from the past provide us with an insight into a certain characteristic of this kind of sight, and that is that it changes our lives. We are different from that moment on. Our lives are different, and our experience of life is different.

I want you to be clear that freedom is not about having beliefs. I have no intention of sharing my beliefs with you. In fact, do not believe anything I tell you. You are encouraged to look for yourselves, to simply look. Freedom is about relieving or ridding ourselves of what restrains us, confines us, and restricts us. It is about disentangling our lives. It is about clearing away the clouds, clearing away the obstacles that prevent us from seeing life as it really is, not as I believe it is, not according to my opinion, not according to my ideas about life, but life as it really is.

On the seventh day of the Buddha's deep Samadhi meditation, as the legend goes, he transcended his thoughts and feelings, awakened and achieved his own enlightenment. What did that mean? Simply that he saw, for the first time, himself and the universe as it really was, directly, breaking through or clearing away the clouds and obstacles in his own life's history that had prevented him from seeing it clearly before. Twenty-five hundred years ago, the Buddha declared that there would be suffering. He spoke about suffering in this way: suffering certainly seems to be an unavoidable and undeniable fact of life. We live most of the time with some level of distress, whether physical, economical, psychological, or social. Many of us have to endure irresolvable situations, painful relationships that will not heal, physical illnesses, disabilities that resist treatment, the constant pain and sorrow of those around us, and the seemingly perpetual agonies of our world. Within this context, what is the possible value of affirming the existence of suffering? In fact, in the Buddha's declaration, "Friends, there will be suffering," we find all of the doctrines, methods of transformation and fruits of freedom.

According to the Buddha, there are four great things that we need to understand about suffering. First: the full extent of its existence. Second: why we suffer as we do. Third: that in reality, suffering is not what we think. Fourth: it is suffering alone that holds the key to genuine liberation. And so once again, we come back to freedom. The Buddha was interested exclusively in the liberation from suffering. These very words imply that suffering is something other than what we often consider it to be. I know that in over thirty years of speaking about suffering, one of the first and almost immediate responses of people when I suggest that life is suffering is a kind of resistance to the idea. "Life isn't just suffering, it is these other things!" But if you were listening to the Buddha's teachings on suffering, you could see that even the most pleasurable things in life eventually, for human beings at least, become suffering.

If we were to refer again to Webster's dictionary, here is his definition of suffering: It is rooted in the Middle English word soffren, which means "to bear up, to endure." Webster's words imply that the suffering in our lives, as the Buddha recognized it, is a kind of manufactured experience that the mind creates in its moment to moment perceptions of life. To be free from suffering, the Buddha said, we must know the cause of suffering. Once you know the cause of suffering, then you simply need to know the causes for the liberation from suffering.

When we look at our lives, we see that they are characterized by the struggles of trying to understand it all from moment to moment. Our lives seem to be made up of desires, disappointments, relationships, and expectations. Looking deeply into his own experience, the Buddha concluded that there is hope. There is hope because there is a cause for suffering and the cause for suffering has to do with the mind. It has to do with understanding the nature of mind and what it is doing from moment to moment. This includes understanding feelings. This includes understanding even the thoughts we entertain in our daily lives and more than that, the feelings and thoughts that manage us in our daily lives.

When we begin to look at the human experience, we find that human beings, in the darkness of the dream-like world that we live in, are managed by feelings and thoughts. People often like to talk about their feelings and thoughts with me. What I often help them to see is that they have no feelings; they have no thoughts. Feelings have them; thoughts have them. When we understand the true nature of feelings, when we understand the true nature of this thinking mind, we can begin to liberate ourselves from suffering. This is another central characteristic or quality of freedom. We have a tendency to surrender our authority to be free over to other beings. We surrender our authority to the government. We surrender our freedom to people in relationships when we believe that if we don't have them, we can't live. We also surrender our freedom to things when we think we need possessions or certain kinds of foods in order to be happy. From the Buddhist perspective, freedom, or to free oneself, is exclusively an individual responsibility.

When His Holiness the Dalai Lama was exiled from Tibet in 1952, the Chinese came with the communist mantra, "We have come to liberate you and the Tibetan people." His Holiness responded, "You cannot liberate me. Only I can liberate me." Freedom is up to you. Liberation is an individual fact. Often I tell my students, you will get out of this practice exactly what you put into it. You get out of life what you put into it. It is vital to understand this on the path to freedom. Liberation is entirely up to you. One of the paradoxes about enlightenment has to do with the fact that there is no guarantee. No one can make you see this. No one can make you free.

No belief can, no person can, no thing can. Only you can liberate yourself. And it is entirely a function of first understanding the tools necessary for freedom, and second, applying those tools effectively in our day-to-day lives.

When we take a look again at Webster's definition of a free person, a truly liberated being, he defines it this way: "a person not determined by anything beyond its own nature of being." That is to say, who I am is no longer a function of anyone's beliefs (including my own) about who I should be and who I should not be. When we look at the mind, we begin to recognize that it is managed by thoughts about life. In fact, whenever the mind is functioning, that is all it is doing. It is thinking about life. There is no factual evidence proved in the mind of any being. There are only thoughts <u>about</u> life. When I am involved in thinking about life, I am also involved in what we will call the "should be" and "should not be" world, the world of duality: the world of good and the world of bad. My life now becomes a function of trying to achieve one objective against another objective. Once again, who I am is no longer determined by my original nature, by who I truly am, but by some idea of who I should be. The Buddha declared that this is where all suffering begins for human beings. He said that the cause of suffering in the world is ignorance, a peculiarly specific type of ignorance: we have forgotten who we truly are.

Beliefs and Feelings: The Golden Calf

Somewhere in your life, somewhere in my life, we forgot who we are. Our lives from that point on become a manifestation of our beliefs, either those given to us by others or those we have set up for ourselves to live by. The truth of the matter is that we are impostors throughout most of our lives. We are always striving to be what others or we ourselves think we should be or should not be, to live by a code of beliefs.

The problem in our society is that beliefs have become the Golden Calf. Beliefs are a kind of idol that the prophets of the Judeo-Christian tradition would point to. We believe that our beliefs are true. A belief is nothing more than an agreement. When I talk about my beliefs, what I am talking about is that I have given my agreement to what someone has told me. That's all it is. There is no evidence or guarantee that what someone has told me is true or not. Webster defines belief as a "state or habit of the mind in which trust or confidence is placed in some person or thing." Take a look at your life. Do not look to me. I have no magic. The answer to your life is exactly where you are sitting. It is always where you are. How much of your life is a function of your beliefs, your agreements with ideas and expectations and opinions of how you should be in life? If you want freedom, you need to create the willingness to look at your life as it is, to look at your humanity as it is.

One of the wonderful things about Zen is that it has no interest in beliefs. When we talk about "shoulds" or "should nots", it does not exist in Zen practice; it does not exist in Buddhism. In Buddhism, there is no expectation of being-ness; there is just what is so. What is so is that there is suffering. No one can deny it. We all experience it directly throughout our lifetime. There is suffering at every moment in life. The only reason why we may not be in touch with suffering is that we are not in touch with our life as it is. We live in a dream filled with beliefs, filled with opinions and filled with expectations, but with no true experience of who we really are. To experience ourselves directly, to see ourselves for who we truly are, to see the universe as it really is, is to awaken to a state of mind that is liberated from all barriers and obstacles. It is to liberate myself from all barriers and obstacles that prevent me from experiencing joy, satisfaction, and contentment in my life no matter the circumstances and situations.

We tend to believe that freedom is the absence of difficulty, that freedom is the absence of pain. If that were so, freedom would disappear. If all of the pain and difficulty in the world were to disappear tomorrow, with it freedom would disappear. Why? Because being truly free does not require some external utopia to be present. Truly free people are contented no matter what circumstances or situations show up in their lives. This is the true definition of freedom. The free person does not act according to anything beyond his or her own nature of being. That is to say, when difficult situations arise, I no longer cease being who I truly am. I am able meet situations calmly and confidently without any sort of diminishing of myself. In fact, because of my state of mind, difficulty shows up not as a problem, but as an opportunity. To be free does not require the people in my life to stop being the way they are; to be free does not require the environment in my life to be different from the way it is. True freedom is the ability to be contented no matter the circumstance and situation at any given time in life.

Webster defines "to be contented" as a function of manifesting satisfaction. This is to say that peace is not something that shows up in my life; peace is something I create in my life from moment to moment. Only the truly free person is capable of creating this kind of peace and contentment. Contentment is something manifested by me. It is the manifestation of satisfaction in my life no matter what is going on around me. No matter how difficult it gets, no matter how joyful it gets, I am able to remain contented no matter the circumstance or situation. In order to achieve this, we must see what the Buddha saw and what all Buddhas have seen since: The true nature of oneself and all the many beings. The path to that lies in seeing the mind for what it is. Why? When we talk about the anatomy of the mind and we take a look at our little minds, filled with thoughts and feelings, we can see that they exist for an exclusive objective and are designed for that purpose only.

It is not for what you think! What I mean by that is that we have become dependent upon our thoughts and feelings in such a way that they have us. They manage us. Once again, you need to take a look at your moment-to-moment experience of daily living. What is your point of reference in your decision making from moment to moment? To what do you refer from moment to moment in making decisions?

When I am honest about the manner in which I live my life from moment to moment, I can see that my point of reference is always either what I think or how I feel. We depend on our feelings in the same way that an addict depends on an external substance. Most of us have come to believe that our feelings are the sacred lamb of our lives. We have come to believe that life is about protecting our feelings. How I feel, what I feel, is essential for my well being. What I want to suggest to you is that my feelings have nothing to do with my experience of well being. Nothing. How I feel from moment to moment does not affect my experience of my own well being. For most of us this is nothing more than an idea. And it is that way only because we have not done the work.

Great strides have been made on the matter of addiction in an effort to understand it: drug addictions, food addictions, and all of the other addictions we talk about. The reality is that there is only one addiction in life and all of the other addictions are nothing more than the manifestation of this one addiction. What is it? We are addicted to our feelings. We rely so much on our feelings that much of our life has been similar to that of an alcoholic or a drug addict. How often do we find ourselves, like the alcoholic or drug addict, feeling helpless because we don't feel like doing or being something or someone today? How many of us are so dependent upon the feeling related to love that we have become addicted to other people? When we look at addiction, we find that all addictions are sourced in the singular addiction to feelings. We are going to take a look at feelings for what they really are.

When you understand what your feelings are, or better, when you understand what the mind is up to in the manufacturing of feelings, then you are able to liberate yourself from your addiction to feelings. Then you are able to act freely. It is my experience that most people have no understanding of the idea of acting independently of their feelings and thoughts. Most of us have no idea what it is like to live independently of our feelings and thoughts. When Webster said that to be free means not being determined by anything beyond one's own nature of being, he included thoughts and feelings in that definition. The Buddha recognized that our original nature neither thinks nor feels. In the Heart Sutra we say no mind, no body, no nose, no tongue, no eyes, no ears and when you complete that whole litany, what you see there is that the senses do not exist in this original mind. For our true nature, the need to reference our feelings and thoughts does not exist. We will take a look at the true nature of feelings and thinking here.

Webster defines feeling in this way: "Touch, emotions, sentiments, affection; a subjective response to a person, thing or situation." At every moment, every feeling I have is a subjective response to some external issue. There's something happening out there. The key to understanding feelings is to understand that all feelings are subjective responses to external circumstances and situations. Webster defines subjective in this way: "Relating to or characteristic of one that is a subject. In lack of freedom or independence; characteristic of or belonging to reality as perceived rather than as independent of mind; relating to or being experienced or knowledge as conditioned by personal mental characteristics or states." All feelings are conditioned, mechanical, learned responses to any given situation. They are a function of the perceived world and as such are not real. When I take my feelings as true at any given moment, I set myself up for suffering, even the most pleasurable feelings. Do not misunderstand me. I enjoy pleasure when it is pleasurable. The difference is that I am not attached to feelings of pleasure. Suffering is a function of attachment to desires. The Buddha said we suffer because of our attachments to our desires.

How often do you feel a particular feeling and immediately you say, "I should not feel that." What just happened in that moment is that the mind and the body are now working together for some idea of life, for some belief of life. To be free is to be independent, to live independently of some belief or idea about life. When we talk about being in the moment, or being present, what we mean is to be truly present to life as it is. One of the things that I often tell people when they come back from a great restaurant and tell me about it is that it's a shame that they never really ate the meal. Most of us don't. What most of us eat is the menu – our idea of the meal. That's one of the reasons why they make those menus so nice looking in really expensive restaurants. Even if the meal is not good, you will not know it. When we talk about the anatomy of the mind, you may come to understand why this happens.

The Anatomy of the Mind

What is the mind? What is this perceiving, thinking, and feeling machine, this egocentric machine? The mind is always egocentric. When I am thinking and feeling, I am in a state of mind called ego. The ego arises when we have come to believe that our thoughts and feelings are real.

The mind constantly perceives the world via the sense organs. It experiences nothing directly. When the mind is thinking, it is formulating an idea about what it perceives. Thinking also implies the unbidden entrance of an idea into one's mind. Feelings are intimately related to thoughts. They cannot be separated. Every moment when a thought arises, all that has happened is that the mind has remembered something from the past and generates a feeling from that memory about the present moment.

All thoughts are preconceptions of the present moment that rely exclusively upon memories of the past. In a way, this is no different from what a computer does. The computer can only provide you with the information it already has. Right now, you think that you are reading my words. I know you are not. You're reading your preconceptions of them. That's why Roshis don't get too concerned about whether students learn or not. I don't mean that to sound facetious or sarcastic; I mean it to sound as it should sound, the way you need to hear it.

Another way to say this is that thoughts and feelings at all times are nothing more than the mind's recollections of the past. The mind is projecting that past situation or memory onto the present moment. For example, when I taste something, I determine the quality of what I am tasting according to my mind's memory of good and bad taste. This explains why some people find certain things sweet and others do not, why some people find certain things pleasurable and others do not. The thing that is in question here is not the objective reality of sweetness or sourness, of pleasure or no pleasure. The preconceptions that we bring to the experience are what that is all about.

The mind is an arrangement of complete multi-sensory records of successive past moments. That is to say that the mind is a kind of data base with complete records of every moment. Through the senses, the mind collects information about its environment. It collects this information and stores it until it is necessary to bring it up.

What the Buddha realized on the day of his enlightenment was that he had spent ten years of his life in search of the answers to the problems about the world. He didn't like the world as it was. He didn't like his world and the world around him. So he went in search as to why the world was so terrible. On the day of his enlightenment, he realized the world was not the problem. The problem was his <u>perception</u> of the world. Perceptions, however, are not innately problematic. Feelings are not innately bad or good. Thoughts are not innately bad or good. Aldous Huxley once said, "Experience is not what happens to you, it is what you do with what happens to you." The Buddha explained that the mind is grasping, attaching itself to external objects. It also attaches recollected thoughts, feelings and opinions about those objects at every moment. My mind refers to past information and delivers its conclusion about the present situation accordingly.

Right now, my mind, your mind is perceiving and recording through the eyes, the ears, the nose, the mouth, and sense of touch. Yet what you come away with in any given situation will be based totally upon what you have brought with you. The mind is constantly looking for agreement. That is to say, it is observing the outer world, referring to the information that it has of past experiences, and comparing what is going on here and now with the past. Many of the arguments that we have had in our lives seem absolutely ridiculous to us in retrospect, don't they? Why? Because they are. Why? Because all upsets are <u>never</u> about what is going on in the moment. To be free is to be aware of that. Why? Why is it important for me to understand that my discomfort at this time really has nothing to do with what is going on in the moment? Why is that so important? Because until I understand that, I cannot truly act freely. I am now acting at that moment in the rage or the anger as a slave being managed by a memory of the past that I have failed to complete in my life.

The mind works according to a simple and undiscriminating logic. The mind is an instrument whose function is to ensure the survival of oneself or of anything that one has come to identify as oneself. The single purpose of this little mind is survival. But here is where the problem comes in. Animals don't have this problem. Humans do. The purpose of mind for humans is whatever they identify as necessary for survival. Animals experience direct survival threats. Human beings generally don't. Why? We eventually come to believe in immeasurable things as necessary for our survival. For example, we come to believe that love is necessary for our survival. And so, we find ourselves in our relationships often arguing about love, don't we? We find ourselves in our relationships ready to go to battle at any moment with the person we love with all our hearts. The only way that we can explain this is to say that in that moment the mind has identified that other person as necessary for its survival. So if you leave me I will not survive; therefore, I will kill you. We've all done it! The mind's singular and exclusive purpose is survival of the being and whatever the being has identified as necessary for its survival. And again, whenever I believe something, that belief is not factual. A belief is not a fact. A belief is an agreement between me and the one who has presented the idea to me. The problem with the mind is that the mind now identifies that as necessary for its survival. Therefore, if there is any threat to the absence of that particular person or thing, the mind goes into survival mode. We call that our fight. We call that worry. We call that fear.

When I ask my students to discover what drives them from moment to moment, fear is the only answer. How much of your life is fear driven? Fear may appear different for you than it does for me, but certainly it is the same thing. When we look at ourselves from moment to moment, we find that the mind is always fearful. It thinks about life constantly because it is protecting itself. Even our smallest opinions about other people are a function of fear. We judge other people, we qualify them, we test and assess them only because we have come to believe that one group of people is good for us and another is not. By these standards, our survival far exceeds mere physical survival. It entails the survival of our ideas, opinions and self-conceptions. This results in making oneself right and others wrong, in dominating and avoiding domination, in justifying oneself and invalidating others. Look at our day-to-day mental activity. This explains why someone disagreeing with us makes us feel so physically uncomfortable. Why do we have such a problem with disagreement in our lives? Why do we feel threatened just because the ones we love might not agree with us? Our opinions -- we all know what they are to us. Someone asks us for our opinion and disagrees with it. What do you observe happening within you?

When I ask the question, "What is the single most important thing to you in your life?" You need to look at what you do from day to day in order to understand that the only answer for human beings is the desire to be right. This includes being accepted by others. That is a euphemistic way of saying, "I want to be right." Being accepted by others makes me the right kind of person, makes me have the right thoughts, and means I am the right person, a good person, and an accepted person. The mind wants to be right and one of the ways in which it does this is by making everyone else wrong. One of the things that you have to understand about this little mind, this ego, is that it is a perfect mechanism. It's perfect. It does what it does perfectly. There's no getting around it. It lacks nothing.

We are always looking for agreement. Most people talk about their friends. In reality, our friends are those who agree with us. Our enemies are those who don't. Look at it. Don't be afraid to look at it because if you don't see these simple facts of our mind's activity from moment to moment, there is no possibility for freedom. If we put off looking at our life, as it is, our experience as it is, our mind's activity as it is, there is no possibility of getting onto the path to freedom. Freedom is the single objective not only of all spiritual practices, but also of the human heart. When people do something irrational, we often say, "Oh, that's just human nature." What I want you to know is that we have it backwards. It is not human to be concerned about what people think about us. That is not human. We have a perverted perception of what it means to be human. When people ask me why I would want to be reincarnated as a human being, I say that the human being is capable of rising above the fears and concerns that manage our lives. You just don't know it because you are deluded by ideas about yourself that have no factual basis. How do we know that you are capable of what I just described? Twenty-five hundred years ago someone did it, and since then, hundreds of thousands have also done it. We are capable of liberating ourselves if we look first at what is in front of us, if we identify the tools necessary for achieving it, and if we apply them. You will get out of this life only what you put into it.

One of the most liberating paradigms shared with me at a very young age was this: the surest way to have your life go on the way it always has, is to continue to do it the way you have always done it. One plus one will always equal two. Sometimes this makes us angry. We want two to not be two. We want two to be three. Or we want two to be four. And we focus on two. We focus on everybody else and everything outside ourselves as the cause of our fear and suffering. And we try to manipulate two. We will try to erase that little line at the bottom and say, "See, it's not two anymore!" But two seems to always come back, doesn't it? Two will always be two in that formula. What we miss is that we need to go to the cause of two. If we want to change two we need to go to the formula that causes two. Our life is a function of formulas. We do things, we say things, and we live in a way that will always produce those particular results as long as we think, do, say and live that way. We cannot continue to believe in feelings and thoughts that are nothing other than the mind's generating the remembrance of a past experience and projecting it into the present.

Let me put this another way. Right now, take a deep breath. Right now, feel what is on your skin. Right now, listen to the sounds around you. Right now, taste what is on your palette. Right now, just observe what is going on in your mind. Your mind has just recorded that experience and stores it in memory and it is sure to represent it to you in the days ahead. Most of you in your adult life are making decisions based upon the way you felt when you were three. You have to see this. So when your mom and dad said to you, "Stop acting like a three-year old," they were on target. How many of us act like three-year olds in our relationships from time to time? Why? Not because there is something wrong with us, but because we do not understand that in that moment, the mind may be bringing up an experience from your third year in life and you think it's going on right in front of you. If there is no clear awareness of how the human mind and body function from moment to moment, the result is division and conflict. This will continue and compound itself throughout our lives if we don't take the necessary steps to correct how we live with our minds and bodies.

To accomplish its purpose, your mind scrupulously records those experiences that are necessary for your survival. How does the mind determine what makes you feel good, what makes you right, what makes you acceptable? Your mind over your lifetime has recorded experiences as necessary for survival and has placed them in a stack labeled "good." Anything that your mind has come to identify as a threat to your survival is labeled "bad."

Right. Wrong. Should. Should not. The mind is a collection of these experiences that is available at any given moment. We summon them up as necessary. The mind contains records of pain and unconscious loss or shock. These are associated with emotional stress and are unwitting reminders of earlier experiences of pain, shock or loss. The most powerful of these records usually relate to our relationship with our parents.

We learn about other people through our experiences with our parents. That is why we talk a great deal in Zen about completing our relationship with them. On the road to manifesting healthful relationships with others, we must complete our relationship with our parents. For instance, we learned about women through our mothers. The infant forms opinions about all the women it will encounter in its lifetime according to its perception of its mother. The single most powerful relationship between an infant and another being is based on its relationship with its mother. There is no other being more powerfully influential on us than our mothers. You may not like hearing that. Some of you may enjoy it. It is none the less true.

Science has proven that we are biologically and not just mentally programmed to respond to the voice of our mothers. You could take a baby and put it ten miles away from its mother. If it could hear her voice, it would make its way back to her. This is certainly not to diminish the influence of fathers. We formulate our ideas about men according to our perceptions of our relationships with our fathers. The earliest data available to us is, if not so obviously, our interactions with our mothers and fathers. Therefore, it follows that the mind reaches back (and I do not want to suggest to you that it stops there) to its earliest parental memories to identify and to formulate opinions about the people it encounters later in life.

Whenever the present environment resembles in any way a painful or stressful memory, whenever one encounters a situation that one perceives as threatening to survival, past memories are reactivated. These memories are called into play in an undiscriminating way as guides. I have had people over the past thirty years talk to me about how they have to get out of their houses and get away from their fathers. For some, it was their mothers. I use fathers because in our society men tend to be, rightfully or wrongfully, the heads of businesses or employers. Years later these same people come to complain to me about their employer. "He doesn't understand me. He doesn't talk to me right. He doesn't treat me as I should be treated." I ask them to remember what they ran away from ten years ago and they say much the same thing. "Well, my father doesn't understand me. He doesn't talk to me right. He doesn't understand how to treat people." You can't run away from this. If you want to be able to work with your employer, complete your relationship with your father.

Whenever the mind identifies something that threatens its survival, it immediately refers to past experiences and memories. It reactivates them in an undiscriminating way, and they become guides as how to avoid pain or threats. You will find that most people are still doing things in the present the way that they were doing them when they lived at home. They do this in their relationships with their lovers, with their husbands, with their wives, with their children. How many men have said, "I want to give my children what my father didn't give me?" That is what all of this is about. What was so wrong about what your father didn't give you? What was so right about what he did give you? It is all in your mind. What you truly are is independent of whatever your parents said you were. Who you are is independent of whatever any authority figure tells you that you are. It does not depend on what your parents think. It does not depend on what your religion thinks. It does not depend on what your society thinks. It doesn't even depend on what you think. It is independent of all the trappings of our day-to-day living. As the Heart Sutra says, "No mind, no body, no thought, no feelings, no eyes, no nose, no ears, no tongue, no memories." Who you are is independent of what you set up in your lifetime as being necessary for your survival.

Our feelings exert a total command over our behavior, controlling bodily sensations, facial expressions, posture, thinking, appearance, fantasies, attitudes, and states of mind. Everything. Our feelings from moment to moment are not limiting just in themselves, but they do limit what we are <u>allowed</u> to feel. How many of us know someone or experienced for ourselves the sense of not being able to feel the love another person has for us? Our beliefs can limit us in ways that literally determine not only what we feel, but what we are permitted to feel. Webster's definition of the word belief or to believe means to fix the limits of any circumstance or situation. Whenever I impose a belief or whenever I define something, one way or another I have limited my experience of that thing. So for example, how many "bad" people could have provided a most wonderful opportunity for us to experience love? Because our beliefs would not permit us to feel this notion even for one moment, we lost an opportunity to love.

Again, our beliefs, our discriminating mind which defines life for us, fixes the limits of our experience. Do your life experiences allow for being loved in your life? Many of us go through life without the experience of being loved, not because it is not available to us but because we have limited our availability to it. I have often asked people, "Do you have room in your life for him?" "Do you have room in your life for her?" Our lives are is so crowded with our beliefs, our opinions, our ideas, our expectations, and our desires, our past and all the people in it, and all the events of the past, that I have to ask you, "Is there enough room in your life for me to come in?" If there isn't, you need to make space. You need to clear and disentangle your mind.

Since the mind operates according to the imposition onto the present of past experience, we see apparent resemblances everywhere. Memories of pain, stress, and pleasure are reactivated continuously. They permeate the present whether or not the resemblance in question is relevant or not. Hardly any present circumstance does not resemble in some way a previously painful circumstance. Everyone is upset all the time in some way. What do we call that in modern society? Stress.

That is what stress is. That is all that stress is. When we attempt to deal with stress, we go directly to the source of it. Meditation is a means of doing this. What are we doing in the practice of meditation? We are causing the mind to leave the past and be present here and now. Why? Because in the here and now there is nothing but possibility. As Bill Gates would ask, "Where do you want to go today?" In the here and now, where do you want to go today? Who do you want to be today? What do you want to achieve today? In the here and now these things are possible. But when the mind's attention is directed exclusively to the past, limitations arise because in the past we find our failures to identify the true nature of being. What is that nature? The Buddha's students asked, "What am I, Lord Buddha?" He said, "Pure potential." Where do you want to go today? What do you want to achieve? It does not matter what it is. When Albert Einstein taught in Princeton, he would go up on the board and write his formulas. Blackboards would be filled with formulas, top to bottom, corner to corner, space to space, and he would ask his students to come up with the answer. They would look at it, as I would look at it, as you would look at it, and he would explain the work this way: "Don't worry. The only difference between you and me is that I've done the work." He knew who we truly are. Do you?

When we define enlightenment, we define it that way. All that happened to Shakyamuni Buddha 2,500 years ago is that he awakened to his true nature. He awakened to who he truly was. In awakening to who he truly was, he saw who everyone else truly was. You see me and everyone else in this room, at this moment according to how you see yourself. If your self concept is one of limitation, one of non-accomplishment, nothing will ever be good enough.

How much of your life is about being good enough? How much of your life is about being better? When the Buddha looked at the suffering in his life, this is what he looked at. He said that suffering is to be expected. The body, by its nature, decays and dies and there is nothing you can do about that. But he went on to understand that most of our suffering had to do with the question, "Why do you worry about these things?" Why do you worry about acceptance and approval? Why do you worry about your quality? Why do you worry about being good enough? Why do you worry about being better? What is that all about? The way to answer that question is by understanding what the mind is doing. Let me review these ideas. The mind, which is a collection of thoughts and feelings, manifests its presence in our body through thoughts and feelings. The mind is active, or at least you can know it is active when you are thinking and when you are feeling. When is the mind not active? Does it stop being active when you sleep? When does it stop being active? As far as you know, when? When you die.

So the mind is always thinking and feeling. It manifests its presence through thoughts and feelings. Are you those thoughts and feelings? Will you at least begin to consider the possibility that you are not your thoughts and feelings, or at least you do not have to be? What are those thoughts? What are those feelings? I have a feeling in my fingertip. I also have a thought about the arm and everything leading up to the fingertip. You cannot feel anything apart from thinking about it. When you take the time to meditate and observe your thoughts, you will notice that when you are thinking something, you are feeling something. Thoughts and feeling are two sides of the same coin.

Every thought you have about life has or brings with it a feeling. Think a thought and a feeling will follow. Every feeling you have about life brings with it a particular thought. If you worry about having particular feelings, you will have the corresponding thoughts. When you identify yourself with your thoughts and feelings, you become a manifestation of those thoughts and feelings. In so doing, you lose your connection with your true nature. You have chosen to become your thoughts and feelings. But who you are is not your thoughts and feelings. Through understanding feelings and thoughts and how they function, we can transform our daily experiences from moment to moment. We call this living mindfully.

For example, if one lives mindfully, one is aware from moment to moment that memories of the past arise continuously. Intimate relationships are the simplest places to see this happening. If I am able to be with my partner, if I am able to be with the people in my life, then I am aware that if an uncomfortable feeling arises, that it is something from the past. I am able to act independently of the past. But if I am not aware of that and act dependently on that feeling, I am simply reacting to the past. That is what most of you are doing within the course of the day -- reacting to life. Stimulus, response, stimulus, response, stimulus, response. If I go to my car and stimulate it by turning the key, it responds. If I go to my coffee maker and stimulate it by pushing the button, it responds. If I go to my computer and stimulate it by pushing its buttons, it responds. When you have come to identify yourself with feelings and thoughts, then the world of stimulus and response prevails. We become machines.

Why is it important to know that? Some of you may think that the answer is to stop being a machine. Another way that we might try to make it work is to change the paradigm of the machine. How many of us cannot get going without stimulation? We need to be stimulated to respond with love. How many of us aren't even aware, that at a particular moment, we are being stimulated by and responding to a past experience. At any given moment, when I am not aware of the mind's activity, I am living in the past. That is why Zen is emphatic about developing the capability of being in the here and now, of being in the present.

"To leave no trace." When the ancients said this, what they were trying to tell their students was to pour themselves into whatever they were doing without thinking of the past, without bringing the past into the present. Many of us have missed the chance for pleasurable opportunities because when the thought of doing them has been available to us, we compare them to past experiences and we don't do them. What we fail to understand is that maybe at the age of three, doing those things wasn't pleasurable, but they could be at the age of twenty. The mind projects your feelings, your beliefs, your opinions, your ideas, your expectations, and your memories, onto every new experience. When I look at a flower, I do not see it. I see my idea of it. Even what I see in front of me depends upon information from the world of stimulus-response.

Filtering Reality

The mind is neither innately bad nor good. It is designed for survival. What happens with us is that we become obsessed with things that are not necessary for our survival. In order for you to survive, we know that you need water. So you've got good reason to be upset about polluted water. Pollute all the water and we don't survive. That's a good upset, if you will. We know that we need a certain amount of food. Here's where the mind goes crazy. When you were a child, someone prepared food for you in a particular way that you enjoyed, even though any kind of food will insure that you survive. I grew up in a Sicilian home. Whenever there was a problem with us kids, my mother gave us cookies. So what do you think my mind tells me to do every time there is a problem in my life? <u>Get the cookies!</u> The monks don't bring cookies home when they go shopping at the supermarket. What was it for you? Where did certain types of food become necessary for your "survival?" How many of us are overweight or have eating disorders only because we do not understand that the mind's singular objective is survival and whatever we have come to believe is necessary for our survival.

How many of us cannot feel the affection of another person because we are still attached to the way in which a parent held us? When we talk about sex in Buddhism, and believe it or not we do, how many of us are unable to enjoy sex all the time? What the mind is doing is comparing everything to that "Oh my God" night. Many people have sexual disorders because they are still looking for that "Oh my God" moment. Forget it. Let it go. It's yesterday, it's an illusion, and it's a dream. If you really want to know love, you've got to be <u>here and now</u> because here and now is where it is. Most of us lose the opportunity to know joy only because we are never present and the things we need for our survival are only here and now. How many of you talk about how the universe is always giving you exactly what you need at any given moment? But you really don't believe that! If you did believe it, then you would not project past experiences onto the present. You would not allow your mind to take over in this way because maybe what you need at that moment is the most difficult thing in your life. In fact, I suggest to you that if you want to be free tomorrow, then imagine the most difficult and frightening thing you could do, and do it.

One of my lessons while growing up happened when we moved to our house in New Jersey and had a pool. Most of us live life like people going swimming. You will notice that when you go swimming, even on the hottest day in the year, you go to the pool, you get in your swim trunks and you get all excited, and you can't wait to get into the pool, and you approach the pool, and what do you do? You dip your toe in. You dip your toe in the pool. All of that excitement suddenly becomes dissipated for you because you dipped your toe in the pool. And one of the things you learn after having a pool your entire life is that the dipping doesn't matter. It doesn't matter. It doesn't change the temperature of the pool. You might be hot, but you're not going to change the pool water. If you just jump into the pool, your caution and discomfort will all be over. It will all be over and now you get to swim and have a good time. But most of us are dipping in the pool. Do you notice how you go back? Well, maybe in a few moments the pool will get warmer. The pool water does not change! So if you really want to enjoy swimming, you need to just jump into the pool. The cold disappears in a matter of moments. Don't worry about it. Now you're in the pool and you are swimming and having a good time and you have no idea how cold it is. The people outside are the ones yelling, "Oh, it's cold! I can't have a good time because the pool is too cold!" And you're in there having a good time.

What immediately happens to you when you get out of the pool? In the pool you don't think. When you get out of the pool you enter thinking and there it all starts to come back in. Worry, worry, worry, fear, fear, fear. Why? Because the mind must be attentive to whatever it has identified as a threat to its survival.

The mind is always looking for agreement. It is formulating its survival mode according to ideas, opinions and beliefs. Ideas, opinion and beliefs are nothing more than formulations of the mind relating to experiences of the past. When we understand that this is the exclusive function of the mind, we now have something to work with. If we do not understand this, then we are nothing more than machines reacting to a particular feeling or thought, which is the stimulus of the body. The body is stimulated according to thoughts and feelings. The mind produces a particular need and we act. Stimulus-response. Our thoughts and our feelings are always subjective. They are never objective. Don't ever ask somebody what they think and assume you've gotten a free and objective response. My students will tell you how often I ask them what they think, which is never. Not only do I not ask you what you think, I don't even think about what you think! You need to see that all thoughts are subjective. All feelings are subjective. Whether or not you describe them as good or necessary for your survival or bad and unnecessary for your survival is entirely a subjective situation for you.

There is something that the mind cannot comprehend, and it is this: The ego is incapable of even comprehending the possibility of functioning independently of thoughts and feelings. It is incapable of comprehending that mode of being. This is why many people fail in Zen practice. They attempt to comprehend Zen through a mechanism that cannot comprehend freedom. The mind is not interested in freedom. The mind is interested in survival. When you think about your life, suffering will follow. When you think about what to do, suffering will follow. When you refer to someone else about what to do, suffering will follow. This is why good therapists do not tell you what to do. They help you to arrive at an understanding yourself. Beware of the Roshi, the monk, the guru, the therapist or anyone who tells you they know what you should do.

There is something else that you need to understand. We talk about all being one. Except in Zen. Zen never talks about being one. There is no such thing as oneness in Zen. We say, "Not two." There is a reason for that. Even though every living being and every inanimate object is made up of everything else you can find in the universe, what is also true about every single one of you and every single inanimate object in this room is this: first (and if you get this your life will work) you are impermanent. You are going to die. You will cease to exist. It will come when you least expect it. And when it comes you will have no say in it and no choice in the matter. Second, when _you_ die, just like when _you_ were born, there never was, there never will be another like you. When you die, you will be gone forever. In your lifetime, even your parents are not you. No one else does things the way you do them. All the Roshi can do is lay out the path. It is up to the student to awaken from his or her dream. Only you can wake up out of that dream. When we look again at Webster's definition of freedom, "Not determined by anything beyond its own nature of being," the path to liberation is in understanding what the mind is doing from moment to moment. The work that we have ahead of us is to discover our innate capacity to be content no matter the circumstances or situations that show up in our lives. That requires a particular way of being that reflects our true nature.

Thomas Merton was a Catholic monk who became so intimate with Zen that when he traveled to Thailand to explore it, some thought he was a Buddhist. He said it this way, "All people are God. The problem is that all people do not live like God." So if you want to know God's experience, live as God lives. You see? He also wrote these words: "A tree gives glory to God by being a tree." Not by being a human, not by being a banana, not by being a squirrel, but by being a tree. By being its own nature. Now, here's the other side. Have you heard the story of the scorpion and the frog? There's a frog at a big lake and a scorpion comes along and wants to get to the other side of the lake. He approaches the frog and says, "Look, I can't swim. If I try it I will drown. Will you carry me over to the other side of the lake?" The frog, being the wisest of all in the lake, says to the scorpion, "Uhhh, no. You're a scorpion. You'll sting me and kill me!" And the scorpion says, "Wait a second! Let's think about this. Why would I do that? If I go on the water with you when I can't swim and I sting you and kill you, I will drown with you! I'm not going to sting you." So the frog does what you do. He thinks about it. Then he says, "Alright, I'll take you across." So they head across the lake. They get about halfway across the lake and the scorpion stings the frog. The moral of the story? A scorpion is a scorpion is a scorpion is a scorpion. You cannot change the true nature of anything. You can disguise it. You can pretend it. But you get what you get because that's all there is to get. You can believe all you want. You can reason all you want. But you get what you get.

To live in harmony with the universe is to understand the nature of the universe and to understand how the many beings manifested by this universe function from moment to moment, particularly the ego mind. I have attempted to give you some insight into how the mind operates, into how it is working from moment to moment. I have tried to give you insight into what feelings are. They are nothing more than manifestations of past experiences. What I am feeling now is like the speed of light. When I look at a star, I am looking at something that happened millions of years ago. When I feel something in this moment, I am feeling something that is the result of something happening before now. You've all had the experience of going home after eating a good meal and had gas. But how many of you decided that the night was terrible because of the gas, even though you were with the most wonderful person you will ever be with? You see. The night as <u>you</u> talk about it will be different than the way <u>she</u> talks about it only because you had gas and you think that the night was about the gas. Feelings are the same way. At any given moment, I must be very careful of deciding what my life is like based upon what I feel because all feelings are a function of something that happened in the past. The same is true with thoughts. The moment I think about anything, I am no longer experiencing the object of my thoughts. I am remembering what just happened and formulating an opinion or an idea about what just happened. You cannot think and experience at the same time. You cannot do it. The moment the mind says, "Wonderful," it is reflecting back to what has happened and attaches to that event or object an idea or a belief. All verbal and written communications about anything are nothing more than that. This is why in Zen, we talk about mind-to-mind transmission. The way the media have often depicted it in films is that when the master recognizes the student is enlightened, there are no words, there is just this kind of understanding.

There is a story about the Buddha. He met in Deer Park with 2000 monks, the first of the religious communities forming around Buddhism at that time. It was there that his successor was identified. The Buddha would not die for another forty years, but at this park he identified his successor. He was expected to give a great teaching on the Dharma. And he did. Upon his arrival, he walked up to the platform and sat down. Everybody expected him to talk about the Dharma. Instead, he reached behind him and picked a flower from the field. He held up the flower, and waited. He noticed a young monk smiling. He had found his successor, Mahakashyapa. The Buddha knew that Mahakashyapa understood this lesson, although no words were spoken between them. If he had spoken, the flower and the Buddha would have died. That's what we do to experiences when we attach our opinions, ideas and beliefs to them.

Artists are concerned with people viewing their art to just see what is there. They are not interested in what people say about it. It's the same with God. I invite you to go and tell God what you think about his world and then let me know what he says. I also invite you to go out and complain to God and let me know when he responds. God is often, and probably always, indifferent to my beliefs about the universe. Experience is like that. When you are in the moment, you know it. You've been there. You've had occasions when you've tasted being in the moment. Maybe you didn't know it. The moment you try to do something with being in the moment, you lose it. I often talk about great athletes doing what they do so perfectly, and how it moves us to watch them. Why? Because athletes will tell you, especially Olympians, that no thought is involved with perfect performances. They fail when they start thinking about what they are doing.

Suzuki Roshi used to talk about experience as being like riding in a train. He said practice is like taking a train from Tokyo to Kyoto. Just sit on the train and enjoy the sights as they go by. But if you look out the window and you look down at the tracks, what will happen? What happens the moment you look down at the tracks from a moving train? You get sick. Thinking is looking down at the tracks. Now, in order to live this way, you need to have a paradigm of life that is independent of thoughts and feelings. I say this in that way because there is a mistake that many people make. Most of the people who come to me have come from a Christian or Jewish background, and as Jews and Christians they talk about how the devil makes them do things. Then they become Zen students and they talk about how the ego makes them do things. So the ego now is the new devil for them. What I want you to know is that our conversation is not about the bad, bad mind. The mind is not bad; the mind is not good. The mind is what it is. If you try to eliminate it, what happens? You continue to suffer. Our practice is to be with our mind and body and the universe as it is. The free person is not one who has eliminated thoughts or feelings, but one who has really learned to be with thoughts and feelings.

Before liberation, feelings have you and thoughts have you. At the moment of liberation, a shift takes place. That's all enlightenment is -- a shift. A paradigm shift takes place where feelings and thoughts no longer manage us. We then are not determined by anything beyond our true nature. What is the nature of that being? Upon his awakening, the Buddha declared it -- all beings are Buddha. All beings. All beings are already enlightened. They just don't know it. The universe is complete and lacks nothing. What does Lao Tzu say to us? "Be content with what you have. Rejoice in the way things are. When you realize there is nothing lacking, the whole world belongs to you." What Lao Tzu is saying is that when you realize everything is complete, including yourself, then you live from pure potential. Then life is about what you want to do today and not what you did yesterday. Who do you want to be today?

The foundation of practice for the Zen Buddhist is that all beings are Buddha. We build upon that foundation. Nothing is lost and nothing is gained. All you need to do is wake up and see this.

Aldous Huxley once remarked that experience is not what happens to you, it is what you do with what happens to you. What do you do with each moment and circumstance in your life? What do you do with that? From moment to moment, what are you doing with the world around you? What are you doing with the circumstances and situations that show up in your life? What is the mental activity of your life? Do you see that what we do with external objects is to evaluate them, assess them, qualify them, test them and so on? Do you see feelings and thoughts as reactionary, learned responses to every given situation in our lives? Our feelings are the response to a particular stimulus, even if that stimulus is as commonplace as, "How are you feeling today?" You will notice that whenever you ask anyone that, immediately they share their feelings or thoughts about their life in that moment. Is there a time in your life when what you are sharing with others is not an evaluation of your feelings or thoughts? This is not a trick question. I want you to look at your experience as Huxley defines it.

The willingness to say, "I don't know," is the first step toward liberation. All assessments about anything, all definitions and descriptions and ideas, all opinions, are manufactured by the mind and are not factual accounts of the moment. In the domain of "I don't know," anything is possible. I can never judge another's experience. I can only recognize it when I see it. But the moment I call it anything, I have lost it. Goodness is a prime example of this trap created by the egocentric mind. Most people try to eliminate the bad in their life by doing good things. You cannot have good without bad. Whenever you think about good, whether you realize it or not, you are also thinking about bad. You can't talk about going up unless you know down. So if both thoughts are simultaneously necessary for the existence of one thought, do you see the duality that the masters talk about? When good is present for us, bad must also be present. If that were not so, you would be contented with good. But what do we do with good?

We try to keep it around. We try to grab it and keep it there. When we make the paradigm shift to "big mind," what is required of us is to become aware of the limitations of our definitions, because the very act of defining something is to fix its limits. Whenever you define anything, you have destroyed your experience of it. This applies even to you. Whatever I say about an experience is not the experience. That's why poets are so weird, at least to those who don't understand their minds. The poet is grappling for some way of explaining the unexplainable to the reader. How do you explain love? How do you talk with someone who hasn't shared your experiences of it? As with the Buddha and Mahakashyapa, there is just the smile.

When I make this paradigm shift in my life there is just experience. The hunger disappears. The craving disappears, the desiring disappears. And I find myself contented with the moment exactly as it is. If you have not seen "The Lord of the Rings," go see it. It is a wonderful picture. There is a great scene between a wise man and his student. Everyone in this particular scene is at a point of great crisis and the student is complaining about why he has to be the one to bear a huge burden. In the dialog he gets to one point in which he starts to judge the moment. At this particular scene, all you have to do is look at the face of the wise man as he turns to the boy. He says to him that even the wisest do not engage in the judgment of others. No one knows the whole story. The Buddha would have applauded that moment. No one knows what any moment really means. To call it whatever you call it is to rob it of the power to transform your life. So just drink the wine. In Zen, we call life the supreme banquet. Just eat the meal. If you want to know love in your life, love the one you're with. Do not worry about how they act. As John Lennon once wrote, "And in the end, the love you take is equal to the love you make." If you want to know love, you don't need anyone. Be a lover. Most of us have no idea how to live like that.

In a seminar I used to give years ago, I talked about the difference between a working relationship and a powerful relationship. If you want relationships to work, all you need to do is find out what your partner's dream is and your partner does the same for you. You spend the rest of your life doing everything you can to empower your partner to make that vision come true and she spends the rest of her life empowering you to achieve your dream. That's a working relationship. If you want a powerful relationship, you've got to give up making the other person wrong.

It is difficult for us to comprehend a way of being that is independent of our thoughts and feelings. And yet, that way of being is possible. If it were not so, then I would not be going on about it. If it were not so, there would be no story about the Buddha; there would be no story about Jesus; there would be no story about Lao Tzu or Mohammed or any of them. Gandhi achieved what no one since him has achieved. He brought down an entire empire. To change India as he did without one act of violence was something unprecedented. When he was asked about his revolution, he said, "This is my revolution: no matter how often the British strike me with the stick, I will not respond with violence." Most of us experience ourselves as incapable of living that way because we have come to believe that our thoughts and feelings are real rather than being nothing more than expressions of past experiences. This requires having a purpose in your life bigger than what you feel and think. When you have done this, you will know freedom. When your life stops being about you, you will know freedom.

When the tea masters of Japan instruct their students to go into the tea house and prepare it for the ceremony, their instruction is to remove everything that is unnecessary. Most of us think that we need the flowers and the tea and the scroll and the ego-based Zen student goes into the tea house and walks around wondering what is unnecessary. Finally he or she goes back to the master and asks, "What do I remove?" Remove everything that's unnecessary for the tea ceremony, the tea ceremony being that place in which two people come together in harmony with one another, removing everything that is unnecessary. "And what is that master?" implores the student. The master says, "Alright, I'll yell you," replies the master. "You!" If you don't believe that, go outside and watch the squirrels' indifference to your presence. When my life is about something bigger than my feelings, my desires, my thoughts, something naturally opens up for me that is not possible otherwise. I enter into God's world, Buddha's world. And in that world, no eyes, no nose, no tongue, no body no mind, no past, no present, no future; everything is just what it is. If all human beings were to leave the planet tomorrow, it would continue on even better than it is now. Why? Think about it.

To Be a Rock in the Tempest

Previously, we examined the cause of suffering as it was defined by the Buddha some twenty-five hundred years ago. Likewise, we examined the causes for freedom as they are defined in Webster's Dictionary. This is not my idea of freedom, not some peculiar Western belief about freedom, but the true and pure definition. When one is free, one has the moment by moment, constant experience of oneself. That experience is not determined by anything beyond one's own true nature. Freedom is the quality of experience or the state of mind when we experience ourselves according to our own true nature. This identification, this true nature, is not to be found in any concept or belief that I might have about life. It, like the nature of freedom, cannot be defined by any limited view of life. And so, in the Zen perspective, freedom is an experience that cannot be explained by the free man or woman. It cannot be given to anyone else and cannot be learned conceptually in any way. When one is truly liberated from the causes of suffering in one's life, it is a function of one's own efforts, one's own work.

Freedom is the state of being free, and to be free is the capacity to live one's life and to experience oneself as not being determined by anything beyond one's own true nature. We transcend the limitations that are seemingly imposed by what shows up in our lives. Freedom enables us to live independently of whatever we are feeling or thinking at any given moment. It is to live independently of beliefs, of ideas, of opinions, of concepts, of the intellectual egocentric mind. This does not imply the absence of these things in our lives.

You need to know that I have beliefs about life. I have beliefs about the way to live life. I have opinions about freedom. I have ideas for my life and for the life of others. So, the idea of enlightenment, or freedom, does not imply the absence of such things. It implies a non-dependent relationship with my beliefs, my ideas, and so forth. A simple way of understanding this is that when my expectations are unfulfilled, I don't lose my bearings. All upsets in life are a function of unfulfilled expectations. When you get upset, all that has happened in that moment is that a particular expectation of yours has not been fulfilled. Our work is to become detached from the results of life.

Certainly we want to work for a peaceful and equal world. In Buddhism we say, "May we strive to live in equanimity and defend with our very lives the equality of all the many beings." But you and I know that we live in a world where that is not so. All the many beings are not held equally by some beings. Certainly we want to work for the freedom and liberation of all beings, but we want to do it in a way that is effective. That way is being detached from the results in our lives. It's like the farmer who throws out the seeds and does everything she possible can to nurture the ground and water the seeds and then eventually, if you know anything about farming, all that's left to do is wait. Either the plant comes forth or it doesn't. If it does, good. If it doesn't, it's not so good. Nonetheless, in the end I have no control over the results. When the Buddha was confronted about this he responded in this way: everything and everyone in my life is of the nature of impermanence. The things I own are of the nature of impermanence; they will rust, they will decay, and they will dissolve. The people in my life are of the nature of impermanence. They will become ill, they will decay and they will die. Everything in my life is of the nature of impermanence. The only thing that I truly possess is my actions, what I say, what I do.

In this paradigm shift, in the domain of freedom, one of the first things from which you must detach is your concern about the way other people are. All that matters to the truly free person is what, despite what is going on, he or she is going to be in this brief time that we have to live. Buddhism teaches that these are the causes of suffering and these are the causes of liberation. You choose. The causes of suffering are not bad, and the causes of joy and satisfaction are not good. Nonetheless, what do you prefer? In this choosing, the implication is that what is important is who I will be in my relationship with others, with how I will relate to life itself from moment to moment. When we have come to identify ourselves or have otherwise become dependent on the mind's activity, on thinking and feeling, there is no choosing. There is only stimulus and response; there is only a mechanical life. We are stimulated by some outside person or thing and respond from a subjective point of view. In the liberated person's life, the stimulus remains the same. Life goes on the way it always has. You can be assured of that. People will continue to be the way they always have been. Things will continue to show up the way they always have. All that has changed for us is that now we are capable of choosing our responses to a particular situation.

What is required for the cultivation of such a being? To this end, we need to understand that all beings who have ever taken on human form have, without exception, been entrapped at one time or another by the mind's activity. Sometime we have come to believe that we are our feelings and our thoughts. The mind is always engaged in thinking and feeling. It manifests its presence in our life through thoughts and feelings. When we do the work of examining the mind deeply, we find that it is, what this egocentric little mind is, is a lifetime collection of information, of situations that have showed up in life. Now that would, in itself, be no problem.

We know that the purpose of the mind is survival. It must be. If you did not have a mechanism for survival, you would last about two minutes in the jungle of life. However, sometime in our lives, we come to believe that our thoughts and our feelings are "real" and we identify our survival with them. When this takes place, the egocentric mind arises. Whenever we talk about the ego, whenever we say, "He or she's being egotistical," what is going on is that the person has come to believe that his or her thoughts, which include opinions, ideas, beliefs and so forth, are who they are. At that point, the mind comes to believe that what is necessary for survival is the protection of those thoughts and feelings. We do this especially for those thoughts and feelings that we classify as being good or pleasurable. We certainly don't try to protect those feelings that are unpleasant. However, I will suggest to you, as I have over the years to my students, that the only experiences in my life that have taught me anything were accompanied by difficult feelings and unpleasant thoughts. This is quite the opposite of what most people think is necessary for liberation. Once we have come to believe that we are our thoughts or feelings, then the mind's singular purpose becomes not only survival of the physical body, but the survival of those thoughts and feelings. All suffering begins here. The origination of suffering is when we come to believe that what is necessary for survival is the protection of our thoughts and feelings.

There are countless reasons for why this misguided drive for survival arises within us. These reasons are unique because we are individuals. All of them, though they may be individual, none the less, rest in one experience. One of the ways I have attempted to describe this is that somewhere in your life, you came to believe the judgments of other people about you. As infants, if you can remember that far back, you were uninterested in other people but they were really interested in you. When you became older, you became really interested in other people and they become less interested in you. Infants are indifferent to what people think about them, aren't they? They do not spend time in the crib worrying about what mommy and daddy think about them. This is the evidence we have that you were not born this way. Therefore, the later responses in life are certainly learned.

Sometime in your life, you become overly interested in what other people think about you. This is when you begin to forget who you are. From that time forward, you begin to take on the actions, the opinions, beliefs, decisions and choices of an impostor, someone whose only purpose in life is to meet other people's expectations. This is when the mind beings to identify its thoughts and feelings as being necessary for survival. This attachment to thoughts, desires and feelings is the origin of all suffering. The indulgence of thinking about life and the quality we give to what we are thinking at the moment is where we find the origin of our suffering. Therefore, it follows that what we have forgotten about our original selves needs to be remembered. A genuine spiritual journey will bring us back to where we began. It doesn't take us anywhere else. We come full circle.

Authentic Spirituality, Zen practice or whatever you wish to call it, takes us on a circular journey. This may be why the dharma icon in Buddhism is a wheel, a circle, pointing out to us that where we are right now is where we will end up on this journey. All that is different is that we will see it differently. This is the objective of any genuine spiritual path. When we look at the definition of suffering, Webster says, "to submit to; to be forced to endure." When we talk about suffering from the Buddhist perspective, we are not necessarily talking about the common pain in the body that comes with old age and illness and eventual death. We are talking about what we do with that pain. In fact, we do something with all difficulties. Suffering is a moment in which we surrender our capacity to rise above the difficulty and instead believe that we are stuck and unable to do anything about it. Webster defines feeling as a subjective response to a person or situation. We understand that all feelings without exception are nothing more than the remembrance of things and the projection of those things into the present moment. Likewise with our thoughts. Whenever we think about anything, we are in the process of comparing what we perceive in this moment with something from the past.

We come back to the definition of freedom, a state of being in which we are not dependent upon our thoughts, opinions, needs and expectations, but are independently living <u>with</u> all those things. A free person can choose an <u>effective</u> response to life. How do we arrive at an answer to the question, "What is an effective response to life?" Another way of arriving at the answer to that question is by asking, "How do I live in a way that produces an effective response?" His Holiness the Dalai Lama says that the purpose of life can be seen by looking at what every living thing desires, which is the desire not to suffer.

When we talk about living effectively, we talk about living our lives in a way that our actions produce liberation from suffering. A trap arises when we indulge the mind's activity and confuse it with our own identity, at which point we experience ourselves as being separate from everything else. Egocentricity is this experience of being separate, unique, apart from all other things. What we need is a formula that will awaken us to our true identity because we know as a fact that the idea of separation is false.

One of the fundamental teachings of Buddhism is the interdependence of all things. Everything is interdependent with everything else. To find my true self, I cannot look in any particular place any more than an eyeball can see itself. Try it and you will realize the absurdity of the endeavor. We must look outside of ourselves, away from ourselves in order to see ourselves. I am empty of an independent existence. Nothing exists independently, including this self that I call myself. In order to know myself, I must know all the many beings. In order to find myself, I must seek out all the many beings.

The entrapment of the egocentric mind is to believe that there is a separate existence. In my own practice over the last thirty years, the only time I experience myself that way is when I am indulging my feelings and thoughts. THE ONLY TIME! If you want to experience love consistently, then you must be a lover. If you are not a lover, you will not have the experience of love consistently in your life. It will not happen. Even if you have the greatest lover in your life, it will not happen for you. I have seen others who have passionate lovers in theirs lives, yet are hungry for the experience of love. The banquet table is always available to them, yet they remain hungry. To love another being is to love yourself. This is why Jesus said, "Love your neighbor as yourself and you will see the kingdom of heaven." The Zen way of saying this is, "Take care of business." Do what is necessary and shut up. When you love someone, stay in the activity of loving, and you will know love.

When do problems show up in your relationships with other people? When your sole purpose is about satisfying your feelings and thoughts or your expectations are not being met. In the process of being related there is no problem. In the process of <u>thinking</u> about our relationships, there will always be problems. The moment I start to think about my relationships, I bring into them my expectations, formulations, ideas, and opinions. Subjective living does not produce life. It kills life. Subjective living gives governments the idea that they have the right to use whatever force they have even at the expense of countless lives to achieve a particular goal in the name of freedom. Subjective living gives societies the idea that they can impose upon nature in any way they want, fulfilling their needs at the expense of other forms of nature. Likewise in relationships, subjective living kills them. Freedom requires having a purpose in life greater than ourselves.

When your actions depend upon results, egocentricity arises. You are still attached. You are still selfish. You want something, but I suggest instead that you love unconditionally. Jesus was asked, "How often do I love my brother?" He said seventy times seventy times seventy. Do the math and what do you get? You don't have enough time in life to forgive that much! What he was saying was to forgive all the time. If your brother takes your shirt, offer him your coat. If your brother steals your car, offer him your house. This is impossible for the ego mind to do. That is why we make impossible vows in Buddhism.

The more you practice zazen, the more you will become aware of how <u>selfless</u> you really are. The selfish being with which you have identified is what you have become. You have yet to rediscover who you have been. That's the problem. You have forgotten who you were before you became a manufactured being. True meditation practice must go through what I call the cemetery. We must go through a menagerie of disguises. It's like pealing away an onion. The more you peel it, the more onion you've got until you get to the center. Once you are there, no onion, just this pure space that was there before the onion came to be. When you first look at this, it is intimidating. Who wants to do this? But the longer you practice, you not only become aware of your selfishness, but eventually you will become aware of your selflessness. You couldn't be selfish if you weren't selfless to begin with because the first thing you gave up was yourself.

If you try to understand this with the mind, that is egocentric, because the ego's purpose is the survival of you and your feelings. You will not get it. What you need is devotion to a purpose bigger than yourself to get this. When you begin meditation, and for a long time thereafter, there is this experience of the self experiencing itself and that's all there is. The longer you stay at it, if you commit to staying at it, what eventually happens is that your true nature starts to emerge. You start to become aware of what seems initially to be another being. It is who you really are. If you really want to do this, you must have a purpose in your life, you must have a way of being in your life greater than just the satisfaction of your feelings and your thoughts. The surest way to have your life go on the way it always has is to keep doing it the way you always have done it. No matter how you disguise it, no matter how you sugar coat it, no matter if you call it religion, no matter if you call it Zen, if whatever you are doing is really about satisfying your feelings and thoughts, you will continue to get the same results. We all do it. There's got to be another way. You can train yourself in such away that you begin to forget yourself and start to experience a greater existence in the universe other than what George Bernard Shaw called, "a selfish little clod of ailments and grievances complaining that world will not devote itself to making me happy."

From the point of view of the ego mind, it's all about me. It's all affecting me and I must protect myself from all of it. Practice, when it is genuine, is what we call, "Everyday Zen." How you cut the carrots, how you wash the dishes, how you clean the toilet, how you make your bed in the morning, how you get up in the morning, is just as important as how you meditate or pray. Meditation will not cure a day of lying and stealing. So if I spend my day not practicing mindfulness and then come home and say that I am going to meditate, usually what is driving me is to feel better so that I feel more peaceful, and that's egocentric, that's desire, that's attachment. This is where the problem lies; we've got to get rid of our "fast food" mentality when it comes to transforming our lives. You cannot pull up to a window and order enlightenment and fries. It doesn't exist.

Pure Consciousness as Pure Potential

In order to rediscover our true selves, we must face what it means to be human and put aside any delusions that would have us try to be angels or otherwise to be free from the demands of the human condition. Zen, unlike many other practices, emphasizes that everything in our life must now become an instrument of liberation. Everything we say and everything we do, how we do it, how we say it and the attitude we bring to it, is essential. You cannot expect to achieve freedom while enslaving others. You cannot expect to achieve your own freedom while living as a slave to anything. Looking at our own experiences, we realize that we live with our feelings and thoughts as enslaved beings. They run us. What else is this but slavery? What else is it but enslavement to thoughts and feelings? And we wonder why our lives are so sporadic and inconsistent. We bring inconsistency to life. First let's talk about the relationship between children and parents. One of the causes of conflicts in child-parent relationships is mixed signals. What will stir a child into destructive action more than anything else? Mixed signals. "I love you, but you've got to become a better person." Mixed signals.

At our birth, all we knew was pure potential. The world was complete. There was nothing but the experience of your mother's loving embrace. There was nothing but the experience of completeness. You cried, the bottle came; you were hungry; the food was there; you were cold; and the blanket was there. Everything you needed in the womb and in those early years of your life communicated to you completeness. Now all of a sudden, you are told you are incomplete. There is nothing more damaging to any relationship than inconsistent communications of unconditional love. Nothing is more damaging than that. We cannot have it both ways. This is why in Zen practice, like any spiritual practice, if you are not prepared to commit wholeheartedly, you will not get the results.

In Japan, there is a tradition among the Roshis to accept students only when they vow to continue the practice and to remain in the practice until they achieve their own enlightenment. With anything less than that commitment, they are not permitted to practice with the community. Possibly Goethe has the reason why:

"Until one is committed, there will always be hesitating. The chance to draw back or retreat always brings ineffectiveness. Concerning all acts of initiative and creation, there is one elementary truth, the ignorance of which kills countless ideas and splendid plans: The moment one definitely, wholeheartedly commits oneself, then providence moves too. All sorts of things occur to help one which never would have occurred otherwise. A whole stream of events issue from the decision, raising in one's favor all manner of unforeseen incidents and meetings and material assistance which no man could have dreamed would have come his way."

You can't con God. You can't con the universe. You've done well conning yourself and others, but we can't con God. We think that the great things of life happen at no price. Every single figure in the history of enlightenment and salvation and liberation has paid a price for freedom. Why do we think we don't have to? You can't have it both ways. And this I believe to be the most difficult gate to go through in Zen. The difference between the students that remain until enlightenment and the students that have come and gone in thirty-odd years has been this issue of commitment. Are you willing to make the commitment to your life that is necessary to achieve your own transformation? If not, go home. I wish you the best you can get. But somewhere in my own life's history, I had to make a choice. I recognized that I could not have it both ways. The universe required for me to fully embrace the work or go home. This is vital.

Are you willing to make the commitment to care for yourself and your life in such a way that will bring about transformation? You will get out of this only what you put into it. If you put your whole heart into it, and full commitment into it, providence will respond likewise. If you give halfhearted commitment to it, providence will respond likewise. Jesus taught his students that what a man sows so shall he reap. What you put out will come back to you two-fold. And this is a level of life that most of us are not even consciously aware of as possible. We have been socially conditioned to be dependent upon everything outside ourselves.

How many of you have bought the toothpaste you use for love? How many of you drive the car you do to be whole? How many of you have the house for completion, and so forth. Our society has taught us that we alone, without the right car, without the right house, without the right this that and this, have no value. Just look at the world you live in. Don't listen to me. Watch the commercials. What are they telling you? What do they say about your body? How many poor souls in this nation suffer on a daily basis because the media say your body makes you less valuable to our society? This is where our beliefs come in. We accept what they tell us as true! We must learn to live in such a way that we are not dependent upon any external stimulus at any given time.

Know yourself as the source of being. This is what God created you to know. This is the purpose of all existence. A tree is valuable as a tree. It doesn't have to be anything else. An acorn is not just an acorn. You put it in the ground and walk away and it becomes a house for hundreds of birds or the very thing you live under. The same is true about you. The Buddha wanted you to understand that who you truly are is not what you feel and think because what you feel and think has been conditioned in you, and every time you attach yourself to your feelings and thoughts, you're just doing what you've been told to do. That's good for children, but not for whole beings. If we do not recognize this, what the Buddha had to say, what Jesus had to say, what Mohammed had to say, what Gandhi had to say, what Mother Theresa had to say has no value to us because that's what all of them pointed to. The Buddha said upon awakening that all beings are Buddha. Nothing is lost and nothing is gained.

Here's where another problem lies: growth and continual change is what you were designed for. If you stop growing and if you stop changing, you die. Growth and continual change is our human vocation. We must give up our fear of change. In fact, if you don't change, you will not awaken because your attachment to the past prevents you from seeing what is right in front of you. The present moment has no trace in the past. This moment is unique, just as you were when you were born. You cannot see that because you keep looking backwards. The Christian and Jewish traditions speak of repentance. Respect is similar. Here is another example of how we have been taught incorrectly. Respect is something that most people use to punish other people, except for Aretha Franklin, who understands what respect is. Repentance and respect means the same thing. Repent means to take a second look, not to jump to conclusions. Those traditions have turned these words into something else, but that is what it means. What do you think respect means? To take a second look. In order to respect yourself, you must look at yourself again and you must ask the right questions. Is all this bullshit true? Is what I have called myself accurate?

If you want to start respecting yourself, which is where you must begin, you must love yourself and have compassion for yourself. Compassion is a function of taking a second look and that is what this practice is about. You get to look again and see what is really there, not what you think is there. In other words, the determination to be ourselves is an essential condition for living life. This is the very opposite of seeking to implement an ill-fitting and irrelevant self-denial. We're all in denial whenever we live according to external expectations and beliefs. The only thing that can be touched deeply is what is real. Everything else falls apart under the pressure of the human heart. The only genuine spiritual experience is rooted in the genuine self. "I and my Father are one." To see me is to see the Father, Jesus said. What was he saying there? Everything is an expression of the original mind. All events, circumstances, and beings have value because when I look at you, I see the Father. When I look at you I see Buddha, when you look at me, you see Buddha. Everything is a manifestation of that. How did you get to be afraid of anything? How did you get to be so worrisome about anything?

Dogen Zenji once spoke of Zen as, "the study of the self." When we look at the mind and we study the self, we find that our responses to life in this moment are learned and conditioned reactions and not based on fact. The spiritual journey is a process, when engaged wholeheartedly, by which one becomes liberated from learned and conditioned living. There are no bad people, there are no evil people, there are no killers, there are no rapists. There are just whole beings that have learned to be evil, learned to be killers, learned to be rapists and so forth. You were not born that way and neither were they. If we do not recognize this, there is no possibility for change.

We must begin our practice by understanding the true and the untrue. What is true is that all beings are Buddha. We are pure potential. What is untrue is what you have come to believe you are. One of the ways of beginning to see this is a rule that I often give to Christians when they come to me for counseling. It's a kind of mantra. What is of God liberates; what is not of God does not. How do I know whether a given choice is in harmony with God and the universe? If it is, it liberates at all times, it sets people free. It sets you free and it sets others free. If you find yourself restricted, confined, confused and suffering, then you are not in harmony with God. When we look at the spiritual disciplines that comprise the Eightfold Path of Buddhism as a model for practice, the first step is right understanding or right view. We have the wrong view of the universe. One of them is that I exist apart from you and independently of you. That's a wrong view, so we need to achieve a right view and live with it. "Life goes on," is a powerful statement. Life goes on. If you achieve something in your lifetime, then life will go on. If you fail to achieve something in your lifetime, then life will go on. So why achieve anything? So that your life will go on. The Tibetans say, "You want a good death? Live a good life." A good death is a function of a good life.

And so it goes that in our-day to-day living, the following is true: you are what your deep, driving desire is; whatever your desire is, you come to believe you are that; as your desire is, so will be your action; as your action is, so will be your future. The laws of the universe reveal that the past, present and future exist in the present moment. What I often bring to the present moment are my experiences from the past. What I am doing in the present moment is laying out the path for the future. So if my desire is selfish, it goes that what I can expect in the future are those things and only those things that are the result of selfishness. Selfishness is one way of living. You can go on being selfish if you want to. But as George Bernard Shaw would suggest, stop complaining about it.

In the domain of selfishness where I feel I have to have things at the cost of others, when it's all about me, I experience insufficiency. For example, if you believe that the answer to your life is in the future, that it is never here and now, if you believe that what you need is in the future and never here and now in the present moment, even when you arrive in the future (which will then be the present moment), will you be satisfied? No. Of course not. Because you have come to believe that you never have enough; therefore, what you need is still to come in the future some time, somehow. Our experience is a function of our deepest desire. Discover what your desire is and if your desire does not provide for contentment, get rid of it.

Forget knowledge and understanding. They don't matter. If you come to know and understand everything in the universe, you get to live life. If you never come to know and understand everything in the universe, you get to live life. We must embrace the mystery that life is. What is the nature of life? It is a mystery. Get over wanting to know it and understand it. You assume that if you knew it and understood it, you could control it. And isn't that what you want? You want to control all of it. It cannot be controlled. Life is bigger than me and you. It cannot be controlled. Can you imagine if human beings could have control over all of life? It's happening, isn't it?

We can see it. We're destroying everything. We're just killing everything off to build what we think life is about. And what we are failing to see is that as we kill the air, we are killing ourselves. We're the scorpion on the back of the frog, aren't we? This need to control kills. It kills the life in you and it kills the life around you. The day you give up control is the day you will have real control and you will be free.

The path to freedom begins with what we call the law of pure potential. The source of all creation is pure consciousness. Whenever we identify something as pure, we mean not polluted by elements other than its true nature. Pure water is water without the pollutants that we put into our streams and rivers every day. Pure potential and primal Consciousness are the same. No eyes, no ears, no tongue, no body, no mind, no enlightenment, no consciousness, none of that exists in the mind of God. God is pure potential -- pure potential seeking expression from the unmanifest to the manifest. When we realize that our true self is pure potential, we align with the power that manifests everything in the universe. When we detach ourselves from our attachment to feelings and thoughts, we then open up the energy that is innate to all forms, all beings, to create whatever we want, to cause whatever we desire. It is because you think you can't do this that you can't do this.

Returning to the Source

Spiritual discipline is the practice of cultivating a seed and nurturing it to fruition. Webster defines "cultivate" as, "to prepare and to refine; to seek, to become one with fruition." When we talk about cultivating the human condition, we talk about preparing the ground for our awakening. That ground, from the Zen perspective, is our everyday living. Zen is a way of life. It is not a system of beliefs; it is not a system of ideas and opinions; it is a way of being. When you look at this way of being, it has been purposefully refined and cultivated over the years by the masters to be nonsensical. It makes no sense; you cannot grab it; you cannot understand it; you cannot figure it out. So, rule number one, and any spiritual practice requires it, the Buddha required it and Jesus required it, is that we follow instructions and take what we get, whatever that is. Another way of saying this is no tile above, no floor below. When we talk about faith, we are not talking about a system of beliefs. The true definition of faith, genuine faith, is having nothing to rely on.

You may have heard the story of a man running through the forest, being chased by a tiger, jumping off a cliff and grabbing onto a branch, hanging there and calling out to God. "God, I believe in you and I believe you are here with me and all of my life I have believed in you, now help me God!" God says, "Well, if you really believe me, then let go." That kind of faith is required here. The Dharma cannot be explained or understood with the intellect. It cannot. It is impossible. The nature of the universe can only be seen; it cannot be explained or understood. Scientists have been trying to do it for how long? They get so far and they come up against a barrier. This is certainly not to diminish science, but rather a fact of life. Scientists will agree with me. There is only so much we can explain and understand and we can go no further. Even any expectation of getting to where you can explain everything is nonsense. But you can know it. And you can know it in a way that when you know it, the need to explain it disappears. You need to set up better goals in your life than you have. Goal number one: have no knowledge of anything. Give up your attachment to meanings in life. No one knows the whole picture. No one can see the real picture. So, in my limited point of view here, that's all I'm going to get to see. There's a big picture here that doesn't care about my limited point of view.

"I experienced my own liberation when I realized the benign indifference of the universe to my complaints." To this end, I give my students an exercise. On a night when the moon and stars are out, go outside and tell the moon what you don't like and the stars what you want. And if that doesn't work, tell God and let me know if he shows up to change it for you. I've never seen it happen. Embrace that. What a wonderful thing. As a very young boy, I once told a priest, "You know why I love God? I love God's arrogance." God does not care about me. We've been best of friends ever since I realized that. Try it in your relationships. Just love the other person and don't care about whether they love you back. Watch what happens.

We want to cultivate the ground for your awakening, your enlightenment. And there is a path, the Buddha said, that does just that. Now this word, "path", is intended for you to understand that you have to walk it. You have to live it. You can't believe this. You can't just believe in God. You've got to relate to God, you've got to interact with God. The Eightfold Path, which is the Fourth Noble Truth in Buddhism, is the way in which we live this. The Eightfold Path has been defined as right understanding, right thought, right speech, right action, right livelihood, right effort, right mindfulness and right concentration. Right understanding or right point of view and right thought are considered the wisdom path. Wisdom is not knowledge. It is a kind of knowing that is a function of seeing directly. So, in the practice of meditation, several things are going on. As the student begins to refine his or her practice of meditation with right effort, eventually the practice becomes something other than just difficulty. One now begins to cultivate, through the difficulty of practice, the ability to look at the universe. And so we have the Bodhisattva's Vow, which begins, "When I, a student of the Dharma, look at the real form of the universe," and it goes on to say what the student sees.

Right understanding begins with making the effort to see what is in front of you, to look at the universe.

When the Buddha saw the real form of the universe, he saw these characteristics: that everything is impermanent; what you have to give up is your idea of permanence; what you have to give up is your indulgence in the need to control. Anything that has life is in constant change, is constantly growing. Growth and change is the only evidence of life. Whenever I try to capture anything in life and keep it that way, I kill it. I kill it. Whenever my life becomes a function of security, and my life is about keeping things a particular way, I kill myself. The life-force within you and me and everything that exists wants to grow and change, wants to become. Now, the paradox is that it is always becoming. Nothing has ever finished becoming. Nothing. So, there is never a time in your practice where you should think you have reached the end. Suzuki Roshi talked about the beginner's mind. He said that seated meditation is not difficult because of the posture and the time required to put into it. Zen is not really difficult because of what is required. It is difficult because human beings don't know how to maintain beginner's mind. What is beginner's mind? It's always living as if you are a beginner, as if all possibilities are open to you. Another way of saying that is this: never think that your life and what you have to learn and grow and become is over. How many of us find ourselves in a constant state of suffering because we don't see that the tragedy at hand is a door, not an ending. Everything that shows up in your life is to be seen as an opportunity.

Marcus Aurelius, an ancient Roman emperor, wrote that, "It is possible to live out your whole life in perfect contentment. True understanding is to see the events of life in this way: you are here only for my benefit, though rumor paints you otherwise." And you know what rumors always generate-Fear: "Ohhh, worry about that! Be afraid of that!" That's what we do in our society.

On a deep level, should we trust everything? When we look at Webster's definition of trust, we find that most of us do not trust others. In order to trust everything in life, you can't have anything to rely on. What if you began to look at life as this wonderful opportunity to start over rather than this horrifying event that you dread? You might become like the Tibetans who never lose anybody because the moment someone dies, they start looking for them in their new incarnation. They never lose anybody. His Holiness the Dalai Lama is an incarnation of Avalokitesvara.

Everything turns to one's advantage when one greets a troublesome situation like this: "You are the very thing I was looking for!" So the next time trouble shows up say, "You were the very thing I was looking for." The next time difficulty shows up, "You are the very thing I need right now." Difficulty is only difficult because we make it difficult. The problem that we have with problems is that we have a problem with problems. That's the only reason problems show up as problems -- because you've got a problem with problems. You think there's somewhere in the universe where there is a rainbow always shining. But rainbows always disappear, and with them go that little Munchkin Land. Whatever arises in life is the right material to bring about your growth and the growth of those around you. It's like relationships in which we are afraid to tell the truth. We always say, "I don't want to hurt their feelings." Well that, first of all, is a lie. That's not why you don't tell the truth. You don't tell them the truth because <u>you</u> don't want to go through the feelings you will have to go through when you hurt their feelings! But possibly that's exactly what you and they need to grow, to become even deeper in love, or more deeply related.

The most difficult circumstances in our life are to be viewed with right thought, right view, right understanding, as opportunities, no matter what they are. Now this doesn't mean you go through these difficulties as if you're in denial. Sometimes it means really struggling with them. We've got to release our resistance to struggling. Childbirth is painful, so why do we think that life isn't? Anything that comes to life, anything that comes to fruition, will be a function of some kind of pain. Even the seed breaking through the ground is painfully breaking through it.

At this point, we might well ask, "How do we use our minds to their best advantage?" The answer to this lies in the Eightfold Path, a system of "right living."

Right Understanding begins with embracing the true nature of life. What is that? That everything is impermanent, everything is in flux, everything is changing. Let your life change and you will experience your own aliveness. Diminish change, resist change, and you will complain about the way life is. You will be upset about the way life is, not because change is innately difficult or wrong or should not be happening, but because we are not in the flow of life. The very thing that gives everything life is change. Right now, at this moment, every cell in your body is changing. Your body is dying. You don't have the same body you had at lunch time! Ask any doctor.

Right view. When we start identifying ourselves as our thoughts and feelings, we then experiences ourselves as something independent from the rest of life, and this causes suffering. When I, a student of the Dharma, look at the real form of the universe, what I see is this: if I travel to the farthest planet in the universe and take a shovel and dig up the soil on that planet, I will find the same things that are on Earth. Everything in you exists in me and on that planet. It may look different over there, but it's the same material and everything depends on everything else. If we continue to kill the forests to build our houses, we will die because without the forests, we cannot live. If we continue to cut down trees we will lack oxygen to breathe. If we continue to pollute the air, where are you going to go and breathe? I need you and you need me and we need everything else -- not as in lack, but because together we make a bigger whole.

Right thought has to do with our attitude. When you achieve right view, attitude becomes transformed, thinking becomes transformed. Something naturally begins to happen in the way you think about others. Thoughts and feelings exist side by side with each other as cause and effect. Think that thought; experience that feeling; indulge them long enough and they will produce similar thoughts. We need to occupy ourselves with right thought. I just described to you one of the right thoughts: love your neighbor as yourself. We need to start viewing the world around us as ourselves. This generates a sense of responsibility to take care of our lives. This begins with me. I need to take care of myself. This involves taking care of my mental attitude and my body. If you continue to eat things that harm you, and you continue to smoke and drink and gamble and do things that harm you, then you will not experience right thought.

Right view and right thought are about seeing the interdependence between thoughts and actions. I think something; I say something; I act a certain way. I now produce a result in the world which is reflected in my environment. When you and I look at the condition of our world right now, we are seeing the state of the human mind. Nothing more. What is going on around you is reflection of what is going on inside you. The laws of the universe require that certain stimuli produce certain results. Love begets love. War begets war. Peace begets peace. Right thought involves entertaining those thoughts that liberate yourself and others and never indulging those thoughts that restrict, restrain or discriminate. Two things happen in my own mindfulness practice from time to time. For instance, when I have an argument with someone I love, two things happen almost instantly. After I get over being upset, I immediately see its source and then act according to a purpose which is greater than me. We need to indulge only thoughts that create freedom for ourselves and others. Whenever a thought shows up in your life that is restrictive or discriminating, do not indulge it.

One of the ways one learns how to do this throughout the day is through meditation. The more you refine and perfect your practice of seated meditation, the easier such thoughts arise throughout the day. Anger shows up; I do not indulge it. Bigotry shows up; I do not indulge it. Hatred shows up; I do not indulge it. Compassion shows up; I indulge that. How do we cultivate this habit of mind? We do it by recognizing that the mind is designed to identify the things that it perceives to be necessary to its survival. If we start indulging thoughts of compassion, then we start indulging acts of compassion. If we repeatedly indulge those thoughts and commit those actions then the mind begins to recognize them as necessary for its survival. In this way, we can cultivate thoughts and actions which generate feelings of joy, satisfaction and fulfillment.

The Buddha said that we use life as it is to cultivate this life-enhancing habit of mind. We start with right view. We know that everything is impermanent and nothing exists apart from anything else; what happens to you happens to me. As the Bodhisattva would say, I will reincarnate lifetime after lifetime until all beings are liberated because no one is truly liberated until all beings are liberated. Why? Not because the Bodhisattva is some special being, but because the Bodhisattva looked into the real form of the universe and found out that you and I are joined at the hip. How do we know this? Look at our world and what is happening in to it. Does anything you see out there cause you to consider that <u>maybe, just maybe</u>, we've got to do things differently? Do you really think the military is going to dissolve the energy that brought about September Eleventh? No. The universe is not designed that way. Just look in the Middle East. It's not designed that way. War begets war. It will always be that way no matter what. Do you think we are going to end poverty in America? Four million children will go to bed tonight hungry. Four million American children will go to bed tonight hungry in the richest nation in the world. Do you think we are going to end poverty by consuming everything for ourselves while others do not have it? Absolutely not. If you think poverty doesn't affect the world economy, you've been sleeping.

The rule of thumb for your spiritual practice is to understand the true form of the universe. If we want to live in harmony with it, we must to give up our control of the things that happen in our lives, the people in our lives, and the opportunities in our lives. Why? Because everything is impermanent. Now, here's some hope for those of you who need hope. If everything is impermanent, then nothing lasts forever. What always follows difficulty? Contentment. What always follow pain? Pleasure. What always follow sadness? Joy. The thing that you don't like is that what always follows joy is sadness because everything is impermanent. Everything is interconnected. If I want to know love, I must be a lover. If I want to have abundantly, I must give abundantly to others. I must take care of myself. I must take care of the people in my life. I must take care of my environment. This is right understanding and right thought. We call this the wisdom path because it directly reflects the real form of the universe. Wisdom is living in harmony with the real form of the universe.

When Avalokitesvara sits around wondering what to do, she doesn't refer to self-help books. She looks at the real form of the universe and responds accordingly. She says, "Everything is impermanent, so I better grab this opportunity right now because in a few moments it may not be here." That is another part of practice. We must appreciate its urgency. You are going to die. You have been given a short time in which to do all of this. If you don't get it done now, when will you?

Right speech, right action, and right livelihood. These are not much different from the first two practices. If I go around calling people bigoted, discriminating, judgmental names, then meditating isn't going to change anything. If I speak angrily and viciously and judgmentally at people, then meditation isn't going to change anything. I must take up the way of practicing right speech. If right thought is what liberates rather than restraining and confining people, then what is right speech? It is speaking only what liberates and not what restricts and discriminates. Right action is the same. Once again, if I put into this body the foods that will kill it, I will die. If I put into this body the foods that will nourish it and enrich it, it will eventually die but it will certainly live a life much better than it would otherwise. It is likewise outside. My actions must be conducive to love. My actions must be conducive for friendship. My actions must be conductive for relationship. If they are not, wake up!

My father was the first Roshi to enter my life. Once, I was beaten up while playing. I was shocked at this. When I got home, my father saw me and said, "What the hell happened to you?" I told him that another boy had beaten me up. When he asked me what had happened, I told him that we were playing ball; I called him a nasty name, and he beat me up. My father said, "Well, what the hell did you think he was going to do!" Right action. Don't be surprised if they beat you up. Don't be surprised if they go away when your actions communicate that you don't care. If you spend enough time with me not communicating your concern for me, I'm going to become disinterested with you too. Right action involves doing those things in life that cultivate life, that nourish life. And what is that? Change and growth.

In your personal relationships, you want to do things that encourage others to be who they are. The more you create the space for people to be who they are and not what you want them to be, they will grow and change. The more they grow and change, the more they will appreciate you. People are going to value you. You know why? Because they don't get that anywhere else. They go to work and they are expected to be one way; they go out to a bar and they are expected to be another way; they want to cry and it's not seemly to cry so they store up all that pain and suffering. You let them cry with you. They'll love you. They'll keep coming back.

Right livelihood. This is one of the most difficult parts of the eightfold path in our modern world, because unfortunately it leaves us with very few possibilities for living the way that Buddha Shakyamuni originally intended us to live. You need to know that in his lifetime he had clear restrictions on who could be monks. He said that people who make weapons for war cannot be monks. Butchers cannot be monks. Tax collectors cannot be monks. If my livelihood, my security, is deliberately harming or killing others; if I am taking from the world for myself while other go without, this is in direct opposition to the true form of the universe. The way of the universe is to cultivate and to nourish in a way that there is enough for everyone. The Buddha was very clear on this. Right livelihood means that we need to look at our jobs. You need to look at your careers. Is what you are doing in any way denying others the same equal abundant possibilities in life?

If we were to travel back twenty-five hundred years, we would see that the Buddha refused entry into his community anyone who made weapons, anyone who sold intoxicants (yes even bartenders could not become monks), and anyone who did something that harmed life in any way. In our modern society, that does not change. We need to take a look at the way in which we pursue our own livelihood. One way we can do this is to become more conscious about what we are buying at the supermarket. In this monastery we do not buy from certain companies that are quite popular in our society simply because we've done the work of investigating other things these companies do.

Right livelihood is not to be received as law, as a rule. Take the case of butchering animals for food. Are butchers practicing right livelihood? His holiness the Dalai Lama ate yak when he was in Tibet. That animal had to be killed to feed him. Not all Buddhists, me included, are strict vegetarians. We are not talking about laws here; we are talking about guidelines for achieving enlightenment. Native Americans, who I think were rather enlightened, also killed animals, but did it in a way that I think the Buddha may have accepted.

When the Buddha was laying on his deathbed, his monks came to him and asked, "What shall we do now?" He said to them, "Rely on yourself. You are the light." This advice will guide you in your issues about right livelihood.

To this end, remember that there is no wrong, no right; no bad, no good; no no-wrong, no no-right; no no-bad, no no-good. You cannot rely on the path of right livelihood to make your decision; you need to rely on yourself. What is so for you? My father is a hunter. Never in my life have I suggested that he stop being a hunter. And I love my father dearly.

Each of us must decide these things for ourselves. Right speech, right action, and right livelihood is the path of morality, not as it is defined as a system of rights and wrongs, bad and good, but as what will produce the particular results we are after.

The last three paths of the Eightfold Noble Path of Buddhism are right effort, right mindfulness and right concentration. This deals with the practice of meditation -- applying right effort to it, applying right mindfulness to our daily living, and right concentration. Why is this so important in the spiritual journey? At the heart of all Zen practice, at the heart of the path that leads to liberation is the practice of zazen or seated meditation. Seated meditation is essential in any spiritual practice in whatever form it is practiced. I say this because I acknowledge the validity of how my contemplative Christian brothers and sisters do it, my contemplative Jewish brothers and sisters do it, the Sufis do it. We Zen students choose zazen. The practice of meditation, right meditation, is essential for any spiritual path. You cannot live ethically; you cannot achieve right view; you cannot achieve right understanding if you do not apply yourself and devote your life to daily meditation. It cannot be done. Why? This is the place in which we attentively and deliberately train the mind. We are transforming its way of being during seated meditation. Right effort is the beginning of that technique. That is to say, we need to apply the right effort.

In the practice of seated meditation, one of the wrong views is that meditation is designed to eliminate thoughts and thinking, that it is designed to push out bad thoughts and bring in good thoughts or that it is designed to achieve some transcendent utopia in our suffering world. This is wrong effort. Right effort begins with the understanding of the Japanese term Shikantaza. Shikantaza is the practice of seated meditation and it is translated to mean, "Just sitting." Just sit in your seat and go for the ride. Seated meditation is designed to bring the mind to an awareness of the true nature of being.

If the mind is discriminating at all times between good and bad, and I am sitting and meditating and my effort is directed toward thinking good thoughts and not bad thoughts, what am I doing? I am reinforcing the ego's view of the world. What is the mind's view? That there are good things necessary for my survival; there are bad things that threaten my survival. I am cultivating duality. I am cultivating a space for dualistic experience. What is dualistic experience? Cultivating a discriminating mind. That's what it already is. We don't want to make it bigger! We don't want to reinforce it and give it more energy. We want to diminish its energy by transforming the mind's view of the universe. And so, when I am sitting, my mind is doing what is designed to do. It perceives my experience in these few moments while I am sitting. Whatever I am doing, my mind is watching, analyzing, and questioning. When the mind observes the being resisting one thing or setting one thing against another, it goes into its designated function of adding to the list of what is necessary for survival and what is not necessary for survival.

In this way, we reinforce the dualism of the mind and we compound the problem. How do we start to turn that around? By just sitting. That is the practice of being still no matter what shows up during our sitting. Even the smallest activity of scratching an itch when it shows up must wait. I have gotten more students angry at me than I can count just by telling them that they cannot scratch an itch. Why would you get upset about that?

Because that is what you do with all discomfort in your life. You want to fix it, or make it go away. Even an itch. Look how quickly you attend to it. The mind recognizes it as a survival threat. It's uncomfortable, it's disturbing, get rid of it. So in the practice of sitting, we're not just talking about those mental formations that show up during those moments that you are sitting, but those physical formations as well. To just sit is to take the posture whether on a chair or on the floor and just sit. Just sit. But what if my toe hurts? Just sit. But what if my knee hurts? Just sit.

I want you to look at how you hold discomfort when you are meditating. You hold it in the same way as if somebody has a gun to your head and is about to shoot you. Because god forbid if you sit with that hurting butt for five more minutes. Why would you want to move if your life's freedom depends upon just sitting? Because the mind is convinced that the pain in the butt is a real threat. That's why. That's why you do the things you do. If we move to take care of the pain in the butt, we reinforce the mind's idea that life is not worth living unless there are no butt pains. That's how you do it. To just sit is to cultivate the opportunity for a paradigm shift. The more and more we give in to the mind's fear of life, the more and more we reinforce and compound the problem.

When we talk about right mindfulness, we are talking about that time of day when we are not sitting and meditating; but it also applies to when we are sitting and meditating. You need to start practicing a way of being by which you become clear about what really is threatening and what is not. What's threatening? No water for a few days. So, when's the last time that happened? O.K. We're safe so far. What's threatening is standing in the street with traffic coming towards you. Is butt itching threatening? Will you die if your butt itches for more than thirty minutes? I don't think so. But if I suggest to you that you are going to have to sit for thirty minutes without moving your butt, you become very defensive, don't you. Very apprehensive and resistant. What's up with that?

So the more and more we respond to that stimulus of the mind to move, we are reinforcing all the other fear-oriented reactions of the mind. It is like saying, "Yes, the mind is giving me accurate information. I am definitely threatened by a butt itch." And this explains why we can't be with other kinds of itches, if you will, in our lives. I will tell you that you should aspire to sit two hours a day, though the quality you bring to five minutes per day can be equal to the quality you bring to five hours per day if you apply right effort. Right effort is not to change things. You are not to try to change the thoughts that show up in your head. Just allow the thoughts to show up. Now, a thought shows up in my head and I start to think about it. Am I sitting? No. Now I am sitting and thinking. So we don't want to think about the thoughts; we want them, as in the image of a train, to just pass by us as we ride the train. Bad thoughts, good thoughts, pleasurable thoughts, unpleasurable thoughts come and go and there we are just sitting. The same thing applies to feeling. When uncomfortable feelings show up, just notice them, recognize them, but don't think about them or try to do anything with them. Practice that for five minutes. When you have mastered that for five minutes, sit for ten minutes. We can surprise even ourselves with how long we can just sit.

You need to know that, when I first started practicing seated meditation, within minutes, my whole body was screaming for help. And when someone told me that in order to even think of becoming a Zen teacher one day I was going to have to sit sesshin for seven days and seven nights around the clock with no if ands or buts about it, I wanted to run away screaming. There was no way it was going to happen. Today I sit for hours on end. It takes a while, but you can train yourself to do it. If we do not expand our reach in life, we will never grow. If we remain isolated in this little capsule we have come to call our safe little world, we will die. All great achievements require the individual to push the envelope. Seated meditation, in the beginning, is disciplining the mind and body until you have become one with your practice of seated meditation.

When we talk about right mindfulness, in either seated meditation or throughout the day, it involves just being aware of what is going on in you and in your body at any given moment. One of the most profound events in my life that best explains what I mean by this has to do with when I was spiritual director about ten years ago at an old Catholic retreat house called St. Francis House of Prayer. It was situated on about one-hundred fifty acres of farmland and I lived on it mostly by myself except for when my assistant was staying over. On the second floor where the bedrooms were there was a full-length mirror. As I walked past that mirror, I suddenly called out for my dad as though I thought he was in the house. This was a profound moment of mindfulness practice. What I eventually realized was that I had seen my father when I walked past the mirror. It was an education at realizing how I had become my father at that time. In the mindfulness practice of life, you become aware of the origination of your thoughts and feelings. This happens only when you stop in seated meditation to observe them. When you watch your thoughts as they show up, you can see where they originate. But if you are resisting some thoughts and only looking at other thoughts, you are not seeing the whole picture. The same thing holds with your feelings. Where does that upset come from? Why do you get so upset about something so little, something so insignificant? What is that for you?

In the practice of mindfulness, not only am I becoming more and more aware of how my thoughts and feelings originate in past experiences, but I also must apply right effort throughout the day. In effect, part of right mindfulness involves being aware of what is going on. For example, in my daytime job, working with monks and lay people, I am surrounded by all different types of people and from time to time I become upset. Right mindfulness involves an awareness of that feeling before I act. There are many times in which I want to act out of anger -- verbally or physically. Right mindfulness is an awareness of that urge or desire or feeling and then acting according to a purpose greater than myself.

When we talk about right concentration as the eighth path of the Eightfold Noble Path, we talk about the practice referred to by the Rinzai master Hakuin Ekaku Zenji as samadhi meditation. Samadhi is concentrated meditation. In order to just observe my thoughts and feelings, I need to apply right concentration. In seated meditation, I may do that by watching my breath; I may do that by persisting in observing my thoughts and feelings and not letting my mind wander. Throughout the day, right concentration is the practice of pouring myself into a task. I don't think about it; I don't think about anything else; I just do it.

I often tell the story of meeting a professional tennis player many years ago. If you've ever been to a tennis tournament, it is a very beautiful thing to watch. Anything, when done by a master, is beautiful to watch. At the end of the tournament, I was invited to a dinner to honor these particular players and I had the opportunity to ask one of them, "What causes the ball to hit the net?" The volley goes back and forth until suddenly the ball drops. What was explained to me is similar to what other athletes have explained to me. When you are in the domain of being, in this case, playing tennis, there is the volley and nothing else. A volley is the action of being a tennis player with no thought of hitting the ball. When the ball hits the net, the tennis player has thought about the ball. So whenever you see the ball hit the net you can say, "Ah, he's thinking about the ball!"

The same is true with you and me. My life's experience has convinced me that when I go to work, and simply do the task at hand, the day goes more quickly and everything flows. The moment I start to think about this stinking task I've got to do, and the people I've got to work with, and the people I've got to talk to on the phone, I never have enough time for anything. Suffering follows. While driving your car, how many of you have driven past your destination and just kept on driving? You missed your turn. How did you do that? You're thinking about something else. But if you drive and think about driving, you get to where you're going.

Right concentration involves training the mind to be present to whatever it is doing at that particular moment. If you are having a difficult time, you need to look at where your mind is. Whenever the mind is not present to what it is doing, the body experiences pain, discomfort, fatigue, weakness, dissatisfaction, and so forth. The body is an instrument of communication. It communicates what is going on in the mind. For example, you may feel exhausted at a given moment when a crisis arises such as a fire. All of a sudden you have all of the alertness you need to escape it. How does that happen? The mind clearly identifies the circumstance as threatening to its survival and pays full attention. Rather than depending upon the mind to do that from moment to moment, we train ourselves to do it from moment to moment. This is what the Buddha meant by right concentration. To concentrate is to stay present with what you are doing from moment to moment.

In order to do this, you need a purpose greater than your life. What I just described to you is the technique. The technique will not work without a purpose greater than the results of the technique. That is to say, if you do this to become enlightened, forget it! The Buddha would say that to <u>desire</u> enlightenment and to <u>desire</u> good feelings are not two separate things. Whenever your action is accompanied by a peculiar desire, you're in a destructive mode of being. One must have a purpose greater than getting anything, greater than desiring. The only purpose that is effective for all beings, human and non-human is to be who you are in every given moment. Now, there's a problem here of which you need to be aware. It's not who you think you are. If you sit there and I ask you who are and you start to spew off all these ideas and beliefs about yourself, you're in trouble. The mind cannot define who you are. It is an experiential understanding only.

Often my students hear me say that the understanding that transcends all understanding is best explained in the instructions to live your life as a benefit to other beings. This is not my philosophy; this is not my belief; this is what can be seen by you if you look. Another way I explain this is to tell a story that someone once told me when we first moved into Pine Wind. "What do think these trees will do if a fire were to sweep through this forest?" Initially the question seemed nonsensical to me. Initially I thought, well, they are all going to die. But what do they do before they die? Do you know what they do? They drop their seeds before the fire reaches them. When they feel the heat approaching, every pine tree in this forest drops its own seeds that it has been holding in the pinecone so that when the fire is over, the seeds have been dropped for new trees to be born in the future. Innately they know to do this. When I heard this, it was clear to me that the ancient teachings of the Buddha were accurate; that everything was created in life to be a benefit for everything else. If I bring that attitude to my daily living, if I sit for the benefit of all the many beings, if I practice patience and compassion for the benefit of others, as do the pine trees, somehow I know that transformation will follow. The pine tree knows when it drops its seeds that even if it dies, it will be reborn again as a new tree.

What is innate to us, and you need to know that you have forgotten what is innate to you, is your interconnectedness with all beings. You can begin this at home. You can begin this at your workplace. You can begin this wherever you choose. And it begins with no evidence about what I've said to you. It has no proof. I cannot prove this to you and I cannot give you a good enough reason. All I can tell you is that my life's experience has convinced me that if you want a purpose that will work in your life, a purpose that will bring about your own freedom, it is to live your life as a benefit for others, to practice right mindfulness in such simple ways as being conscious of turning off the light when you leave a room, of being conscious of the products you buy at the supermarket. Before I eat, I am mindful of all of the beings who gave their lives for me to enjoy this meal, and I give thanks. I am grateful. There is a small prayer that I say without failure before I eat my meals. "I am grateful. May I be worthy to receive you." May my life be worthy to receive what you have done for me. You will then be able to transform what you eat when you begin to eat it for the purpose of continuing to practice the Dharma; so that you may live as a benefit for others.

Little things like that are beginnings. Eventually what happens is that everything becomes your concern naturally. Suddenly a squirrel becomes much more than a rodent. Suddenly the stars are much more than just stars. Everything begins to change naturally including what I see when I look in the mirror. This is a consequence of forgetting yourself and living your life as a benefit for others. If you are willing to bring that attitude to the practices I have just described, by living your life as a benefit to liberating others, then you will find your own liberation.

Glossary

Avalokitesvara: The bodhisattva of compassion.

Beginner's mind: The innocence of one's first inquiry into the nature of being; openness to doubts and possibilities. An essential practice of the Zen mind.

Bodhi: The perfection of essential nature. Actions issuing from bodhi-mind have the inherent dignity and purity of Buddhahood.

Boddhichitta: Another term for bodhi-mind.

Boddhisattva: Any being who has attained enlightenment and vows to lead all other beings to their enlightenment.

Bodhisattva's vow: Four promises to: a) liberate all beings; b) transcend passions no matter how numerous; c) penetrate Dharma gates no matter how numerous; d) attain the way of the Buddha.

Dhammapada: A collection of 423 verses containing the Buddha's essential teachings.

Dharma: A word with layers of meaning ranging from the laws that govern the universe to Buddhist doctrine.

Dharma Wheel: Symbolic representation of samsara, the continuous cycle of birth and death.

Dogen Kigen (1200-1253): The founder of Soto Zen in Japan who promoted shitkantaza, or just sitting, as the practice of enlightenment.

Dokusan: A private meeting with a Zen master for purposes of individual instruction.

Gassho: The joining together of the hands, palm to palm, to express gratitude and respect.

Eightfold Path: The practices of right understanding, right view, right thought, right speech, right action, right livelihood, right effort, right mindfulness, and right concentration.

Hakuin Ekaku Zenji: Japanese Zen master who revived Rinzai practice and systematized the koans.

Heart Sutra: Also known as the Prajna Paramita Hridaya. Prajna Paramita means "the wisdom that leads to the other shore." The theme of the Heart Sutra is "form is no other than emptiness, emptiness no other than form."

Kensho: A first awakening to one's true nature and thus the nature of all existence.

Kokoro: The "heart" or essential nature of something.

Koan: An enigmatic statement, which cannot be solved by reasoning.

Mahayana: The "greater vehicle"; one of the two main sects of Buddhism. A means for realizing one's own enlightenment for the sake of others.

Metta Sutra: The Buddha's words on kindness, intended to awaken transcendent wisdom and the heart of compassion.

O-Rohatsu: A retreat (sesshin) held in December to commemorate the Buddha's enlightenment.

Paramita: The perfection or culmination of certain practices.

Samadhi: A state of intense absorption in which identification with individual thoughts and feelings are transcended in favor of deep, illuminated awareness.

Samsara: The cycle of birth and death, with its attendant delusions; reincarnation.

Sangha: A community of people practicing the Buddhist ways. One of the three "jewels" of practice along with the Buddha and the dharma.

Satori: A fundamental transformation of character resulting from insight into the truth behind dualism and discrimination

Shakyamuni: Literally, the silent sage of the Shakya clan. An honorific eventually applied to the historical Buddha, whose name was Siddhartha Gautama.

Shikantaza: A mode of zazen that involves neither koan practice nor the counting of breaths.

Soto Zen: One of the two dominant Zen sects in Japan, the other being Rinzai.

Sutra: Literally, "a thread on which jewels are hung." Written teachings and dialogs that purportedly issue from the Buddha himself.

Tathagata: A name used by the Buddha when referring to himself as one who has come like prior Buddhas.

Three Jewels: The three foundations of Zen practice – the Buddha, dharma, and sangha.

Zazen: Literally, sitting Zen, in which the mind is one-pointed and not distracted by random thoughts and feelings.

Zendo: The room reserved for formal sitting practice, considered the core of any given Zen center.

Breinigsville, PA USA
21 June 2010
240283BV00001B/6/P